Adolf Hitler

A PHOTOGRAPHIC DOCUMENTARY

First English edition published by Colour Library International Ltd.
© 1983 Text: Colour Library International Ltd. 99 Park Avenue, New York, N.Y. 10016 U.S.A.
© 1983 Illustrations: Keystone Press Agency, London and Central Press Agency, London, England.
This edition published by Crescent Books
Distributed by Crown Publishers, Inc.
h g f e d c b a
Display and text filmsetting by ACESETTERS LTD., Richmond, Surrey, England.
Printed and bound in Barcelona, Spain by LLOVET and EUROBINDER.
ISBN 0-517-40561 X
CRESCENT 1983

Adolf Hitler

A PHOTOGRAPHIC DOCUMENTARY

Ivor Matanle

Designed by Gary Hazell
Produced by David Gibbon and Ted Smart

CRESCENT BOOKS

Contents

On November 8th each year after the Nazis came to power in 1933, the party hierarchy commemorated the Putsch of 1923 with a march through Munich to the Beer Cellar. Here Hitler is accompanied by Goering, Frick, Knibel and Weber.

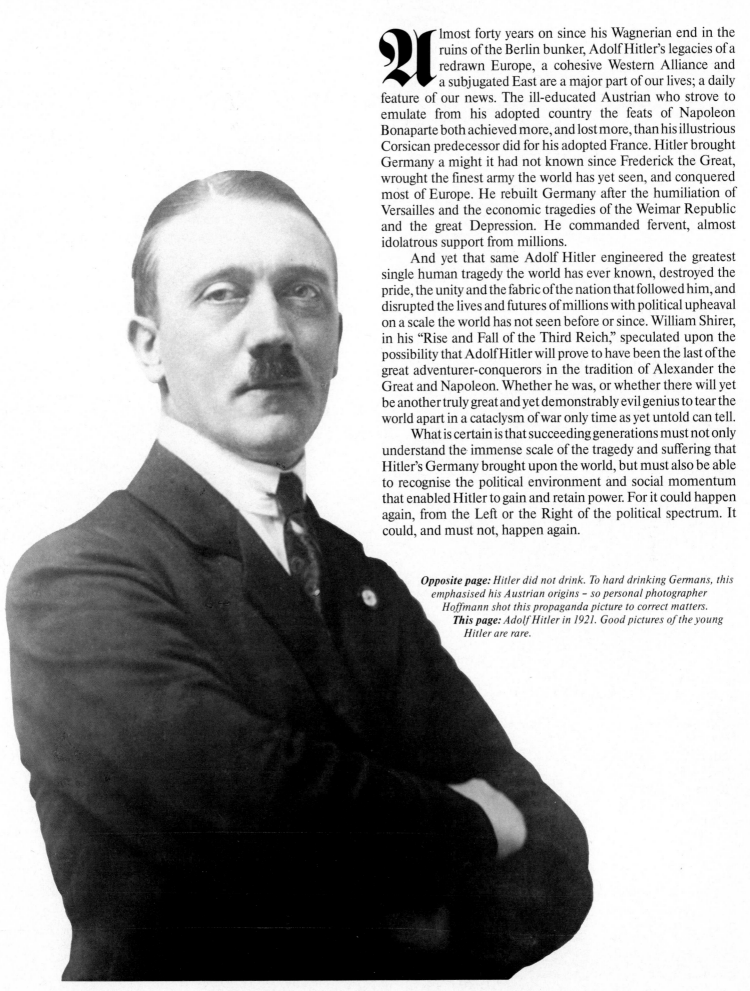

Almost forty years on since his Wagnerian end in the ruins of the Berlin bunker, Adolf Hitler's legacies of a redrawn Europe, a cohesive Western Alliance and a subjugated East are a major part of our lives; a daily feature of our news. The ill-educated Austrian who strove to emulate from his adopted country the feats of Napoleon Bonaparte both achieved more, and lost more, than his illustrious Corsican predecessor did for his adopted France. Hitler brought Germany a might it had not known since Frederick the Great, wrought the finest army the world has yet seen, and conquered most of Europe. He rebuilt Germany after the humiliation of Versailles and the economic tragedies of the Weimar Republic and the great Depression. He commanded fervent, almost idolatrous support from millions.

And yet that same Adolf Hitler engineered the greatest single human tragedy the world has ever known, destroyed the pride, the unity and the fabric of the nation that followed him, and disrupted the lives and futures of millions with political upheaval on a scale the world has not seen before or since. William Shirer, in his "Rise and Fall of the Third Reich," speculated upon the possibility that Adolf Hitler will prove to have been the last of the great adventurer-conquerors in the tradition of Alexander the Great and Napoleon. Whether he was, or whether there will yet be another truly great and yet demonstrably evil genius to tear the world apart in a cataclysm of war only time as yet untold can tell.

What is certain is that succeeding generations must not only understand the immense scale of the tragedy and suffering that Hitler's Germany brought upon the world, but must also be able to recognise the political environment and social momentum that enabled Hitler to gain and retain power. For it could happen again, from the Left or the Right of the political spectrum. It could, and must not, happen again.

Opposite page: Hitler did not drink. To hard drinking Germans, this emphasised his Austrian origins – so personal photographer Hoffmann shot this propaganda picture to correct matters.
This page: Adolf Hitler in 1921. Good pictures of the young Hitler are rare.

The overwhelming impressions left with those who saw, heard and met Adolf Hitler in the thirties are of the almost magical power over a crowd of his oratory, the intensity of his gaze, and the theatricality of his approach to important meetings and public appearances. We know from the accounts of his staff and associates – and to some extent from his own diaries – that Hitler rehearsed his speeches and their presentation thoroughly. This set of pictures by Heinrich Hoffmann, shows Hitler in 1925.

The story goes that after his release from his nine-month stay in Landsberg Prison, following the abortive beer cellar putsch, Hitler wanted to capitalise on the considerable propaganda success at his trial in 1924, so went to see Hoffmann. A record of one of his own speeches was put on the gramophone, and while his own voice boomed and thundered around the studio, Hitler struck the appropriate attitudes and adopted the expressions that he thought right to get his words over. After he had studied the pictures, he ordered Hoffmann to destroy the negatives. Fortunately, Hoffmann disobeyed.

In speeches early in his career, Hitler balanced the ranting with which he became associated with quieter, more persuasive speaking.

The years of obscurity. ■

When Alois Hitler's youthful third wife (and second cousin) Klara produced their third child on the 20th April 1889, there was no reason to suppose that the latest inhabitant of Braunau am Inn, just across the Austrian border from Bavaria, would follow in the steps of Bismarck, the Hohenzollerns and Hindenburg. Alois Hitler was an insignificant customs official, born out of wedlock, and, although his parents had married not long after his birth, was legitimised to bear his father's name only when he was thirty-nine, before which he had been known by his mother's name of Schicklgruber. Young Adolf's mother was twenty-three years younger than Alois, and had earlier borne Gustav and Ida, both of whom died in infancy. The next child, Edmund, died when he was six. Only Adolf and the fifth of the family, Paula, survived to adult life.

Adolf Hitler's childhood was less than happy, although not totally insecure. He did well in his first school, but failed dismally to sustain his early promise when he moved on in 1900 to the High School in Linz. There he failed to get his certificate and was eventually obliged to move to a lesser school in Steyr, to the considerable displeasure of his domineering father, who wanted him to be a Civil Servant, and had no time for Adolf's professed intention to become a great painter. Hitler frequently expressed a very low opinion of his teachers who were, in his assessment, responsible for his early failure.

Alois Hitler died in 1903, and young Adolf left school in 1905, still without a certificate. In 'Mein Kampf' (My Struggle), the interminably tedious tome that Hitler dictated while languishing in Landsberg prison in 1924, he describes the period from 1905 to 1908 as "... the happiest days of my life ... almost a dream." Despite his mother's considerable hardship and lack of money, he made no attempt to work, read voluminously, developed his lifelong love of the music of Richard Wagner at the Linz Opera House and became obsessed with politics and hatred of the Hapsburg monarchy. This idyll was disturbed only by his failure to be accepted by the Vienna Academy of Fine Arts, whose adjudicators dismissed him with the words "test drawing unsatisfactory," and advice to try architecture; counsel which could not be put into practice without a school leaving certificate.

Hitler was still smarting from this rejection when, in 1908, his mother died. He wrote "I had honoured my father, but my mother I had loved." Perhaps with more sincerity he also wrote "I was faced with the problem of earning my own living." In 1909 he went to Vienna and began what he liked to term "the saddest period of my life." From then until 1913 "Hunger was my faithful bodyguard," a condition which he seemed unable to associate with his unwillingness to turn his hand to honest toil. He lived rough, first on the open streets and then in a doss house, and walked the streets unshaven, in an old black overcoat and hat, selling watercolour copies of pictures of Vienna where he could and dispensing anti-semitic political diatribes to anyone who would listen.

During Hitler's early years in politics in Bavaria, his meetings were often poorly attended and frequently in the open. He was personally very short of money, and the same seedy raincoat appears in countless pictures of the period. In this picture, taken in 1923 when he was becoming famous in Germany against the background of the struggle between the Bavarian and the Central governments, he is seen with Rosenberg (left) and Dr Friedrich Weber of the Oberland Freikorps.

Left: *The extraordinary fluke photograph that captured the joy of the then unknown Hitler in August 1914 as he listened to the Bavarian Government's proclamation of war in the Odeonsplatz, Munich. Days later, he was in the army.*

Below: *As success began to come in politics, Hitler retained his common touch and his understanding of the mood of the people that was a crucial factor in his rise to power. On his many chauffeured trips around Germany in the supercharged Mercedes he could not afford, he frequently stopped to meet people and be photographed.*

Opposite: *Meetings of the Nazi Party leaders were frequently held at the Berghof, Hitler's mountain retreat. This picture is undated and almost uncaptioned, but the dress suggests that it was taken at one of these weekend gatherings. Left to right front row, Heinrich Himmler, Dr Wilhelm Frick and Hitler, with Hermann Goering at extreme right.*

In 1913 he moved to Munich, apparently to avoid Austrian military service. But his adoption of the spirit of his new Fatherland was such that, just over a year later, a rare photograph, preserved by chance, shows him amidst the crowd in the Odeons Platz, listening with glittering eyes to the Bavarian government's proclamation of War. Two days later he applied for permission to join up, and was welcomed into the 16th Bavarian Reserve Regiment. Hitler was undeniably a brave and successful soldier who saw himself as fighting selflessly for an ideal he held high. His comrades could not abide his humourless aloofness, but he was twice decorated, even winning, in August 1918, the Iron Cross First Class, which was rarely awarded to ordinary soldiers.

Beginnings in politics.

Above: Hitler reviews the SA as they march past. This picture is strangely symbolic, almost surreal in the isolation of the figure. The location is Frottmaninger Heath, Munich, the time 1923. The figure on the right is Graf.

He heard about the armistice of November 1918 while in hospital recovering from being gassed in the final battle of Ypres. Hitler was shattered; appalled. "Had they died for this?" he wrote. Almost a year later he swallowed whole, as did most of the beleaguered population of Germany, Hindenburg's assertion that the "German Army had been stabbed in the back," despite the then suspected and later proved fact that Hindenburg and his army staff colleagues had repeatedly urged the Armistice upon Kaiser Wilhelm II. In the ten months since the armistice, Bavaria had seen a Social Democratic 'People's State' under Kurt Eisner, and, briefly after Eisner's assassination, a soviet republic, put down in May by one of the volunteer and illegal *'Freikorps'* of regular troops, sent from Berlin. Power all over Germany was effectively with the Reichswehr – the Army – and with the conservatives and monarchists who loathed the Social Democratic government that clung tenuously and almost unwillingly to power in Berlin. *Freikorps* groups were springing up all over Germany; the nation was divided, leaderless, ashamed. The Army sought desperately to maintain national spirit and put down the forces of revolution.

Nationalism was brought to fever pitch by the terms of the hated Treaty of Versailles, which Hitler, and most of his adoptive Bavarian compatriots, saw as a betrayal. Munich became a centre of *Freikorps* activity, attracting nationalists from far and wide to its beerhalls and political meetings. Hitler was still in the army, and had been posted to the Press and News bureau, where, given the

opportunity to address meetings, he discovered for the first time his great gifts as an orator, and learned the first lessons of propaganda. In January 1919 came a fateful invitation to join the German Workers Party, a small and as yet powerless talkshop group under Anton Drexler. There he met Ernst Roehm, a tough professional soldier, later to play a significant role in Hitler's rise. He made speeches, took over the party's propaganda, built its following and, at the party's first major meeting on February 20th 1919 at the Hofbrauhaus, enunciated the famous 25 points of National Socialism, hastily cobbled together by himself and Drexler the night before.

This speech demonstrated for the first time a characteristic that Hitler was to show again and again – the capacity to spell out, clearly, totally repugnant policies, and yet be completely ignored by those who might have been expected to oppose him. The speech proposed the union of all Germans in a greater Germany – a fair warning of the annexation of Austria and the demands for the Sudetenland and the Polish corridor. It stated that Jews were to be denied office and citizenship. It proposed the abrogation of the Treaty of Versailles. And the last of the 25 points postulated the "Creation of a strong central power of the state." As in Mein Kampf, Hitler gave fair warning of unfair measures.

On April 1st 1920, the party's name was changed to 'National Socialist German Workers Party' – the Nazi Party was born. At the end of the year, with funds whose origin is far from clear, the party acquired an ailing twice weekly newspaper, the *Voelkischer*

Above: Hitler in contemplative mood at an SA rally on Frottmaninger Heath, 1923.

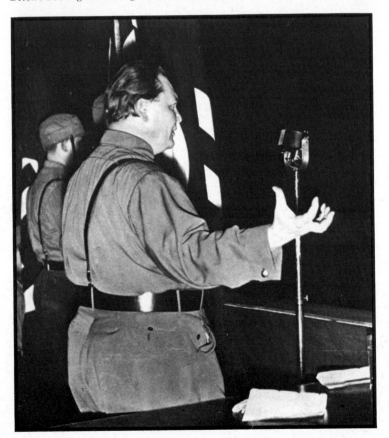

Below: Goering addressing the SA, about 1930.

Beobachter, later to play a major role in the development of the Nazis' political powerbase. Rudolf Hess joined the party. And in the summer of 1921 Adolf Hitler, now clearly the leader of the party, spoke for the first time in Berlin. As events gathered momentum, Hitler designed the infamous red, white and black swastika flag; Hermann Goering, a First World War fighter ace, and last commander of the famous Richthofen Circus, joined the party, and Goering and Roehm organised the *Sturmabteilung* – the Stormtroopers, whose brownshirted men were to be led by Goering into many a skirmish after he took command in 1922. Other henchmen – Rosenberg, the self styled intellectual of the party, the loathsome Julius Streicher – joined the party, and its numbers grew to thousands.

In the Autumn of 1921, France decided to take a firm line over Germany's non payment of reparations, and, following a request from the German government in Berlin for a moratorium on payments, occupied the Ruhr, Germany's industrial heartland. German nationalism was given a further boost, and a massive campaign of passive resistance by civilian workers in the Ruhr brought industry to a virtual standstill. In February 1923, the four main armed patriotic Leagues of Bavaria joined as one organisation under Hitler, and in September Hitler scored a major propaganda triumph by being beside General Ludendorff, a war hero and nationalist not famed for his logical approach, at a mass meeting in Nuremberg of the *Deutscher Kampfbund,* the German Fighting Union.

Above: *General Erich von Ludendorff, one of Germany's greatest First World War heroes, and Hitler, apparently together, but actually as two separate photographs montaged together. Ludendorff refused to have anything to do with Hitler after November 1923, when Hitler first fell flat then ran in the face of police gunfire after the Beer Hall Putsch.*

Below: *A 1923 picture of Hitler with General von Ludendorff (centre, on Hitler's right). Ernst Roehm, later commander of the SA, but at this stage still an army officer, is on Hitler's left.*

Right: *The funeral of General Erich von Ludendorff, at the Feldernhalle in Munich on December 22nd 1937. Hitler was present, but uncharacteristically refused the opportunity to deliver an oration, since the prejudices of the dead General about political leaders who ran away under fire were well known. In 1919 it had been Ludendorff who, with the reported inadvertent assistance of a British officer, coined the expression that the German Army had been 'stabbed in the back' by the Armistice of November 1918, and thus provided a basis for dissatisfaction with the Weimar government upon which Hitler capitalised.*

All this was against a background of mounting economic disaster. Seeking desperately to meet demands on its resources by printing ever more paper money, the Berlin government fuelled an already savage inflationary spiral. In 1921, the dollar had been worth 75 marks. By January 1923, the mark was 18,000 to the dollar, by July 1st 160,000. By November, it took 4 billion marks to buy one dollar. Savings were wiped out, middle class prosperity evaporated.

Three days after the German Fighting Union met to proclaim its nationalistic indignance in Munich, a State of Emergency was declared by Chancellor Stresemann and President Ebert in Berlin, and the Bavarian government followed suit with its own defiant State of Emergency under Gustav von Kahr. The power in Bavaria now rested with Kahr, with General Otto von Lossow, commander of the Reichswehr in Bavaria, and Colonel Hans von Seisser, head of the Bavarian state police. The people, the Army and the government of Bavaria seemed united in their objective to overthrow the Berlin Socialists. Hitler believed, not for the last time, that his moment had come.

Right and facing page: Hitler, accompanied by Goebbels, speaking during one of the election campaigns of 1933.

Below: Sixty thousand political leaders swear an oath of allegiance to Hitler in the Berlin Lustgarten.

Hitler addressed a huge crowd in the Berlin Lustgarten during Mayday celebrations on May 1st 1933. Later that day he announced to a crowd of 1.5 million his plan for a new Germany.

Hitler leaving the Siemens works after speaking to the workers.

Hitler loved to affect Bavarian dress. Here he is with SA stalwarts (left to right) Schab, Schrech, Maurer and Schneider. Note the autographs.

In fact, as October 1923 wore on, the Berlin government showed signs of reasserting its hold on power. The immediate threat of Marxist revolt was past, and, although the Bavarian ruling triumvirate continued to refuse to act on orders from Berlin, they also became less inclined to believe in the wisdom of direct action. But for Hitler there was no drawing back. His newspaper, *Voelkischer Beobachter,* attacked the Berlin leaders viciously, and the Minister of Defence ordered Kahr to suppress the publication. Kahr refused. The Minister went behind Kahr's back to Lossow – who also refused. On October 20th, Berlin dismissed Lossow, but Kahr announced that Lossow would remain in control of the army in Bavaria, and asked for an oath of allegiance from the army to Bavaria, in defiance of the Constitution. By the end of October, the armed Freikorps bands that supported Kahr were massing on the borders of Thuringia, and Hitler was congratulating himself on a neat piece of subversion.

But still he had to use the situation to gain power for the Nazis. He had inspired his supporters to believe in the success of immediate Nazi revolution; he knew that, if he did not act quickly, his followers would be disillusioned and all his earlier political success would be wasted. His was an all or nothing situation. Kahr was constantly reassuring the *Kampfbund* that together the trium-

virate and the *Bund* would conquer Berlin, but was in fact more inclined simply to opt for independence – a separatist viewpoint. When Seisser returned from a visit to Berlin with the conviction that Northern Germany would not support an uprising, the Triumvirate told the Kampfbund that it would not march on Berlin. Hitler decided to force their hand.

An initial plan for the SA to surround the triumvirate and Crown Prince Rupprecht during a parade on November 4th fell through, but a revised plan was drawn up for a march by the entire forces of the *Kampfbund* on 11th November from Frottmaninger Heath into Munich, sweeping Kahr, Lossow and Seisser into open revolution on a wave of public enthusiasm. As this plan was discussed, the triumvirate announced that a big meeting was to be held on the night of November 8th in the Burgerbraukeller, and that Kahr would speak. Believing that Kahr was about to announce the independence of Bavaria, and the restoration of the Wittelsbach monarchy, Hitler decided on the spur of the moment to embark upon revolution at the meeting, and so forestall Kahr and his presumed bid for independence.

Twenty-five minutes after Kahr began to speak, with Hitler languishing unnoticed in a corner, Hermann Goering burst into the hall at the head of twenty five armed stormtroopers. Hitler leapt on a chair, fired a shot in the air, and announced that the

Above: Hitler and associates pelted with flowers at Nuremberg in 1929. Note the characteristic pose of Julius Streicher, later Gauleiter of Franconia 1933-1940, at left of the front row.

Above: Hitler visiting one of the Nazi party districts in 1929. The others are (left to right) Graf, Hess, Schaut and Steinbinder.

National Revolution had begun. "This hall", he claimed, with almost total disregard for the truth, "is occupied by six hundred heavily armed men. No one may leave the hall." He told the people at the meeting, who had no idea to what extent he was bluffing, that the Bavarian and Reich governments had been removed, and the Army and police barracks occupied, and that troops and police were marching on the city under the swastika banner.

There were in fact six hundred SA outside, and a machine gun had been positioned in the hall. Hitler had also arranged for Frick, who was still a police official, to phone the police at the meeting and tell them not to take action. He was therefore able, after his brief oration, to leave Goering in charge out front, and to shepherd Kahr, Lossow and Seisser into a side room. Scheubner-Richter was despatched to collect General Ludendorff, who was to be the figurehead of the revolution, although nobody had in fact thought to tell him of this beforehand.

It was at this point that things began to go wrong, and Hitler's scheme seemed to be coming drastically unstuck. For, far from welcoming his revolutionary initiative and falling in joyfully behind the swastika, the triumvirate sat silently and refused even to talk to him. Hitler ranted, threatened to take his own life, tried everything. Finally, in desperation, having achieved nothing with Kahr, Lossow and Seisser, he rushed back into the hall and on the spur of the moment announced that the three leaders had agreed to serve under him in a new German government, reeling off as he did so an impressive list of ministerial appointees.

The effect was magical. The crowd roared its approval, and the triumvirate, still in the back room, were impressed. When Ludendorff, who had now arrived, advised them to join with Hitler, they returned to the hall and each made a speech of support. Hitler followed these speeches with a stirring oration, and the entire assembly broke into *Deutschland uber Alles*. Hitler was overwhelmed. He thought his destiny was about to be fulfilled. Believing that there was now no turning back, for him or for the triumvirate, Hitler left the hall, and thereby committed a grave error that was to cost him dear. For, once he had gone, his new colleagues faded into the night, and forgot about the revolution until morning, by which time, like a proposal of marriage at a party, it did not seem such a good idea after all.

The whole night passed without important positions being seized, other than the occupation by Roehm of the War Ministry, and without any major development. By morning, Hitler had thousands of men under his command, but little idea of what to do next, and had lost contact with Lossow. Kahr had issued a proclamation denouncing the promises of the beer hall, and things seemed to be disconcertingly normal. The conspirators were at a loss. So, fearing inaction, they marched with General Ludendorff on the Ludwig Bridge in the centre of Munich. Shortly after noon, the column encountered in a narrow street a cordon of police who were not inclined to give way. Shots were fired. The shooting lasted only a minute, but Goering was badly injured, Scheubner-Richter was killed, and a total of sixteen Nazis and three police were killed or injured. Only General Ludendorff and his adjutant stayed on their feet and kept marching. Hitler lost his nerve, got to his feet, and retreated to a waiting car. He was arrested two days later at Uffing.

Left: The Beer Cellar Putsch centenary in 1933 was a special one – the first since Hitler came to power. Here Hitler is acclaimed by Stormtroopers of the SA on 10th November 1933. Notice Goering in the back seat of the Mercedes in which Hitler is standing.

Hitler with a group including Roehm, Himmler and senior naval officers.

Prison and the wilderness.

Above: Hitler with Gregor Strasser, Weber, Schwartz, Amann and Graf at the Hofbrauhaus.
Below: The ill-fated Captain Ernst Roehm, later Commander of the SA, in 1919.

itler's remarkable political talent was demonstrated as never before by the way in which he turned the disaster of the Munich putsch in November 1923 into a political triumph by April 1924. His handling of his twenty-four day trial was magnificent. The press reported his harangues word for word; the public listened to his damning accounts of the duplicities of Kahr, Lossow and Seisser and agreed that they were as guilty of treason as he. Hitler used the trial to reassert his support of the Army; to urge the cause of nationalism; to reinforce his position as natural leader of the disaffected. He was sentenced to five years imprisonment, of which he was to serve only nine months.

In the early summer of 1924, over forty National Socialists were locked up in Landsberg Prison, fifty miles from Munich. Hitler used his comfortable sojourn to dictate the massive and almost unreadable *Mein Kampf,* whose only virtue is the accuracy of its predictions of Hitler's policies when he came to power. While he was in prison, his appointed deputy Rosenberg and other party members scored a minor triumph in the State elections, and the *Voelkisch* bloc became the second largest party in the Bavarian parliament. But Hitler feared for his own position in the party, and railed against Rosenberg's success, and against Roehm, who, although convicted of treason, had been released the day the trial ended. He did little to sustain public support for the party that relied almost totally upon his charisma for its success.

By the end of 1924, support had fallen away, and the Reichstag elections were a disaster for the party. Hitler, accurately, predicted that he would need five years to build the party up again.

A youthful Dr Josef Goebbels in 1934.

Ten years after the Beer Hall Putsch, in the year of his achieving power, Hitler marches at the head of the '1923 Heroes' in Munich. Goering is on his right. Notice the hand cranked newsreel camera being operated in the background!

In February 1925, after the departure from the party of Roehm, Strasser and Ludendorff, Hitler relaunched the Nazi Party, with only those prepared to accept him as undisputed leader numbered among its members. At the end of 1925, the Locarno Pact removed some of the fuel from the fire of German Nationalism. France withdrew from the Ruhr, and Germany, France and Belgium agreed to respect existing borders and refrain from the use of force. At the beginning of 1926, the British Occupation troops pulled out of Cologne, and in September of that year Germany was admitted to the League of Nations. By 1927, the Republican government of Stresemann had restored order, achieved a stable monetary system, and was negotiating an honourable settlement of the reparations problem. New economic disasters were on the horizon, but there was every risk of Germany's population becoming complacent.

A further contributor to civil peace was the coming in April 1925 of Hindenburg to the presidency, Ebert having died in February. Hindenburg was approved of by the very conservative and military elements who had so profoundly disapproved of Ebert and Stresemann, and reconciled the conservatives, at long last, to the republic. Hitler recognised this, and had thrown the Nazis' support behind Hindenburg in the election. This shrewd, if uncharacteristic move was the first step towards Hitler's respectability and national acceptability; the first true step towards power.

But Hitler's problems were a long way from being over. He was banned from public speaking in Bavaria until May 1927, and in Prussia until 1928, and was improvident, extravagant and perpetually short of money. He relied exclusively on his earnings from writing articles, and on his royalties from *'Mein Kampf'*, the first volume of which had been published in 1925, after extensive rewriting to make it less unreadable by an improbable-seeming anti-Semitic priest named Stempfle. Yet, despite his lack of funds, he had bought a supercharged Mercedes, employed Rudolf Hess as his secretary and even employed a chauffeur, as he could not drive himself. In 1928, Hitler rented a villa on the Obersalzberg, which he eventually bought, renaming it the Berghof. His widowed half sister (Alois' daughter by his first wife) Angela Raubal came as his housekeeper, bringing her daughters, with the elder of whom, Geli, Hitler fell madly in love, probably for the only time in his life.

Enthusiastic acclaim for Hitler after he finally became Chancellor – this picture was taken on the 18th May 1933.

The original caption reads 'Hitler and his dog at the Fuehrer's mountain home.' The picture is undated, but appears to be from about 1934.

Issued to counter reports of revolt, this picture of 30th June 1934 shows (left to right) Franz von Papen, General von Blomberg, Hitler, Goering, and Goebbels.

The original caption on this shot says it shows Hitler at a May Day youth rally in the Lustgarten, Berlin. There is no date, but it is probably in 1937. Hitler's Iron Cross, which he always wore with pride, is evident.

The rise to political achievement.

eanwhile, the Nazi Party was growing again under the energetic guidance of Gregor Strasser. The SA remained independent and unwilling to submit itself to party discipline and control, a situation which caused mounting friction between Hitler and Roehm. At the first Nuremberg Party day in August 1927, 30,000 SA men were on parade; by now, Nazi Party membership was 72,000. By 1929, that number had risen to 178,000 and the SA was beginning to be outnumbered tactically in the power echelons of the party. Himmler had left his chicken farm to join Hitler in that year, and took over the SS, at that time numbering only 200 hand-picked men. By 1930, the combined forces of the SS and SA numbered well over 100,000 men, a greater number than the Reichswehr itself. Sensing that the road to success stretched before him, Hitler set about creating a mighty party organisation, capable of marshalling a far greater membership than it had at that stage of its development. The country was divided into 34 gaue, or districts, each with a gauleiter (district leader). Seven more gaue were defined for Austria, the Sudetenland, Danzig and the Saar – a taste of things to come.

Goering had returned from Sweden to Berlin in 1927, and

Hitler was soon back in touch with him. In May 1928, both Goering and Goebbels were elected as Nazi members of the Reichstag – Hitler could not stand for election himself because, as an Austrian, he was ineligible. But in the rising economy, with more jobs and food, and better living standards, the mood of the population was not on the side of political agitators. Another approach was needed, and Hitler's sometimes remarkable feeling for political undercurrent detected what that approach should be.

Hitler knew that the temporary economic stability and growth was shaky and on poor foundations – Germany's borrowings were huge, and her planned economy gave little scope for industrial enterprise, a situation typical then as now of all countries obliged to endure the universally equal misery of socialism. Hitler saw that the wealthy industrialists needed hope of economic freedom and growth, and would support with cash whoever promised that freedom to them in a credible manner. So he set about projecting the Nazi Party as the party of free enterprise and industry, with considerable financial success.

Then, in 1929, came Hitler's first major chance to walk the national political stage. Stresemann died in October 1929, shortly after persuading the French that their final withdrawal from

An undated group, believed to date from 1933. Seated is Dr Frick, then left to right, Goebbels, Hitler, Roehm, Goering, Rosenberg, Himmler and Hess.

An early picture in the beer cellar – Hitler and Ritter von Epp.

of the Weimar Republic was hopelessly divided and incapable of strong government – in 1930, ten parties polled more than a million votes apiece. Government was a tissue of shaky coalition, which the slightest disagreement could topple.

In September 1930, the Reichstag elections saw campaigning by the Nazis on a scale as never before. The result surprised even Hitler. The Nazis, who had in 1928 polled only 810,000 votes and won 12 seats, received nearly 6,500,000 votes and took 107 Reichstag seats, becoming the second strongest party in the state. The Communists also gained, achieving 77 seats, an increase of 23 over 1928. But it was Hitler's hour. He was now a major politician, whose success was welcomed even by the Daily Mail in London, as a bastion against Bolshevism. By the end of the year, the membership of the Nazi Party was almost 400,000.

In 1941, almost twenty years on from the picture on the left, Hitler addresses his old comrades of the Beer Hall Putsch in Munich.

Germany should be linked to agreement to the Young Plan, an American led scheme for future German reparation payments. But, although the French accepted Stresemann's terms, the still nationalistic German people did not. Hitler was able to project himself, albeit alongside a nationalist bigot and former director of Krupps named Hugenberg, into the national limelight as one of the leaders of the campaign to urge rejection of the reparations settlement plan. Hugenberg had access to big industrial money, and Hitler subjugated his dislike of his new ally to his liking for the economic benefits of alliance.

President Hindenburg finally signed the hated reparations agreement in March 1930, but the preceding battle had lent Hitler and the Nazi party such credibility that the Weimar Republic would never be the same again. By the end of 1930, Hitler had the financial support of Emil Kirdorf, a major industrialist and leader of the German mining industry, and used the money to which he now had access to give the party a style to which it was entirely unaccustomed. The Barlow Palace in Munich was taken over, redecorated and used, as the Brown House, to entertain visitors in positively regal splendour. Political campaigning and leafleteering reached new heights. With a membership approaching a quarter of a million and growing fast, the Nazi Party seemed unstoppable.

Even greater impetus was added by the coming of the Great Depression, whose effect hit Germany, as it did the other industrial nations, during 1930. The economic disaster that ended the rising financial and monetary fortunes of the Weimar Republic coincided with the political disaster of the reparations agreement issue. Germany, with her huge burden of debt, was savaged by the Depression to a greater extent than almost any other Western country. The Reichstag under the electoral system

Through 1931 and 1932, the party prospered as the economy foundered, unemployment mounted, the SA grew and engendered ever more street violence, and the political might of Nazism built towards the climax of power. The vast and growing machine of districts and cells stretched across the country, and was administered by a complex bureaucracy headed by a committee of six – Hitler, Strasser, Roehm, Goering, Goebbels and Frick, who became both the first Nazi Minister and the leader of the Nazi Party in the Reichstag.

Hitler now found the 25 points of National Socialism, enunciated so long ago in the Hofbrauhaus, somewhat embarrassing, since he relied for much of his party's funds on those very industrialists whom some of the 25 points threatened. It took all his guile to prevent the more idealistic among his political flock from propounding ideas in the Reichstag that would destroy his source of money. The Republican government of the new Chancellor, Bruening, was propped up by the army, and the by now extremely old President Hindenburg, aged 84, was supported increasingly by Major-General Kurt von Schleicher, a shadowy figure whose name, appropriately, means 'intriguer' in

Hitler arrives for an extraordinary meeting of the Reichstag at the Kroll Opera House, Berlin, July 1934.

German. Schleicher was a friend of Hindenburg's son, and through him had become close to the President. He had also attracted the notice, early in his Army Staff career, of General Groener who, when he became in 1928 the first Defence Minister appointed from the Army by the Weimar Republic, appointed Schleicher as his right hand man. By 1930, Schleicher's influence had grown sufficiently for him to be able to convince the President to appoint Bruening to the Chancellery. His power was thus considerable.

Schleicher formed the notion that the power of the SA could in effect become a reserve for the army, still limited by the Treaty of Versailles to 100,000 men, and that the strength of the Nazi party could be brought in to support the government from the inside rather than destroying it from the outside. He and General Groener supported Bruening's and Hindenburg's contention that, although the excesses of the SA should be checked, they saw no politically acceptable way of checking them. Thus, by adopting a policy of short-term expediency, the government assisted Hitler in his task of bringing them down. By putting

Bruening into power to rule by Presidential decree, and without benefit of parliamentary approval, Schleicher had in fact been too clever by half – he had, for the first time, put the Army into a position of subordination to the President and Chancellor as a power in the land.

At the beginning of 1931 Hitler came to an agreement by which, in return for the lifting of a ban on Nazis working in army and some other government establishments, he reaffirmed his support of legality by publicly issuing an order forbidding the SA to take part in street fighting. Roehm, eager to curry favour with the army, complied, and the disorder in the streets that was causing so much political disquiet died down. Hitler's stock rose, and by the end of the year, Schleicher was seeking Hitler's support for the re-election of President Hindenburg when his term expired in 1932. The way was now open for Hitler to edge into a position of bidding for a role in government; for a share in the coalition that the Weimar Constitution made inevitable. And the winning of 230 out of 608 Reichstag seats in the July 1932 elections gave him that opportunity.

Left and below: *These pictures taken at the Berlin Sportpalast in 1933 show something of the spirit and enthusiasm of countless SA and Hitler Youth rallies at the famous Sports Palace in the thirties. Thousands of young hopefuls of the Hitler Youth were inspired by Hitler's oratory.*

Above: *An earlier occasion at the Sportpalast, in 1932, when Hitler took the salute at a meeting of the Stahlhelm – the 'Steel Helmets.' On his left is Prince August Wilhelm, son of the ex-Kaiser.*

44

Above and left: Despite difficulties with the SA, Hitler recognised in the Stormtroopers the basis of his strength until he came to power.

The Stahlhelm, or Steel Helmets, although rivals of the SA and politically antipathetic to Nazism, became reluctantly part of Hitler's strength against the Weimar republic. This Stahlhelm parade of 150,000 men took place on 4th September 1932.

A picture dating from about 1929 of Hitler, Hess (behind, on his left) and Roehm with other SA leaders.

In October, Hitler had his first audience with President Hindenburg – just three weeks, incidentally, after the suicide of Geli Raubal, his sweetheart. The meeting with the President did not go well, and for that and other reasons associated with Hugenberg's reactionary attempts to establish a 'Harzburg Front' to bring down Bruening, Hitler refused to support the re-election of the President. The next three months saw much political manoeuvring, culminating at the end of February in Goebbels being able to announce in the Berlin *Sportpalast* that Hitler was to run for President against Hindenburg. Hitler was in fact still Austrian, and still ineligible, but, three days after his candidature was announced, he got himself appointed 'an attache of the legation of Brunswick in Berlin.' Reminiscent of Gilbert and Sullivan's madder moments, this ploy made him automatically a German citizen, and campaigning began in earnest.

When the results were announced, Hitler came second with 11,339,446 votes, 86% more than the party had polled in 1930. Hindenburg was first with 18,651,497 – but Hindenburg was 0.4% short of the absolute majority he needed under the Constitution, because two other candidates had polled 7.5 million between them. So a second election was called which, on April 10th, with one fewer candidates, gave Hindenburg victory despite Hitler increasing his poll by over 2 million votes. During the campaign Roehm and the SA had over-reached themselves several times, not least by cordoning off Berlin on the day of the first election with the evident intention of launching a coup d'etat if Hitler won, and the power of the SA and SS made Bruening and Schleicher nervous. Once Hindenburg was safely back in power they had him sign a decree suppressing both the SA and the SS.

At first the Nazis were devastated, and Roehm and Goebbels were keen to do battle with government and the army. Hitler was cleverer, and recognised that there was more to this situation than met the eye. He resolved to let events develop, which they speedily did in the form of grandiose intrigue by Schleicher. When the SA was proscribed, at his suggestion, he persuaded Hindenburg to write to Groener, the Defence Minister, complaining that the Social Democrats' private army had not been similarly suppressed. The resulting row culminated in Groener's resignation. Bruening was next on the list. Schleicher secretly proposed that, if Hitler would accept control of the SA by the army, and would become a part of a Presidential cabinet ruling without parliamentary consent, the proscriptions upon the SA and SS would be lifted, and Bruening would be ousted with Hindenburg's support. The deal was struck, and on Sunday May 29th, Hindenburg asked for Bruening's resignation.

Contrast the visible power of Hitler's entourage at the Nuremberg rally of September 1933 with the pre-Chancellorship picture on the previous page. Hess is now in the black uniform of the SS.

A rare 1933 picture of Hitler in a top hat, with von Papen (left) and General von Blomberg.

But the constitution required there to be a Chancellor. Schleicher persuaded Hindenburg to ask a man whose inappropriateness for the task was total, even laughable. Franz von Papen was not a politician, not a member of the Reichstag, had failed as a minor diplomat, and was noted for his incompetence in everything he attempted. On June 1st 1932 he became Chancellor. The Reichstag was dissolved, the ban on the SA and the SS was lifted, and elections were called for July 31st. Set free to run riot, the SA pillaged and murdered on a scale never before seen. In Prussia alone between June 1st and 20th, there were 461 pitched street battles, eighty-two dead and four hundred wounded, and it got worse as time went on. In the face of mounting street violence, Von Papen banned all parades from mid-July, and appointed himself Reich Commissioner for Prussia in place of the elected government. Martial law was proclaimed in Berlin, and the Socialist ministers were arrested for failing to accept their fall from power.

Hitler saw all this as the beginning of his opportunity finally to bring down the Republic and seize by force the power that had eluded him at the ballot box. Yet, with his henchmen, he campaigned for the elections as never before, determined to preserve his front of constitutional legality, drawing huge crowds to his public meetings. Despite Hitler's promise to support von Papen, Goebbels attacked the Chancellor in every speech he made. When the results of Germany's third national election in five months were announced, Hitler and the Nazis had scored a resounding victory with 13,700,000 votes and 230 out of 608 seats in the Reichstag. Party membership was now over a million, the SA and SS together numbered 400,000, and Hitler was the most powerful man in Germany. But he still lacked a majority in the Reichstag.

The SA, apparently as a result of post-election anti-climax, went on the rampage again. By mid-August 1932, the Nazi leaders realised that Germany's industrialists and people were fearful of what a Nazi government might do. On the brink of success, Hitler saw a risk of losing everything. He was between the devil and the deep blue sea. On the one hand, he could not risk losing the support of the SA by accepting less than total power. On the other he was uncertain whether total power was attainable without first accepting coalition. And his money supply relied upon the goodwill of industry, whose confidence was being daily more shaken by the SA. Until he moved the SA would continue to cause riot. A rapid resolution of the dilemma was imperative.

On 13th August, Hitler met General Schleicher and von Papen in Berlin, and was offered the Vice Chancellorship. Papen saw no reason to stand down for Hitler, who did not command a majority, and who was regarded by Hindenburg as decidedly odd. Hitler flatly turned down the Vice Chancellorship, announcing that nothing less than the Chancellorship would do. He raged, threatened, told Papen and Schleicher that days of mass murder in the streets would surely follow if he did not become Chancellor. Papen and Schleicher were shocked at his uncontrolled behaviour, but remained adamant. Later that day Hitler was summoned to the President's palace and received a dressing down for breaking his promise to support Papen, following which a Government press release ensured that the world knew that Hitler had come off worst.

By November, following the failure of political manoeuvres by Goering, who had become President of the Reichstag in August, and the dissolution of the Reichstag by Papen, Germany was once more in the throes of a General Election. This time

Hitler lost ground, for the first time in years, finishing 2 million votes short of the Nazis' previous figure, and with 196 seats out of a reduced total of 584. The Communists gained sharply with 100 seats. Buoyed up by Hitler's setback, Papen again attempted to get Hitler into government; again Hitler refused. Schleicher suggested an attempt to divide the Nazi Party by hijacking Strasser into government; Papen refused; Schleicher announced that the Army no longer had confidence in Papen. The result was Papen's dismissal and Schleicher being asked by a saddened Hindenburg to become Chancellor.

The Fuehrer in Weimar, apparently in 1933, although the picture is not dated.

Thus the final act of the Weimar Republic began. Throughout January, Papen made overtures to Hitler for a deal by which he and Hitler together might overthrow Schleicher. On 15th January, the Nazis won an important propaganda victory by gaining a majority in the state elections in Lippe. Schleicher continued to approach Nazi leaders for collaboration in the hope of dividing his enemy. He failed every time. By the 22nd January, feverish negotiations were in progress by which Hindenburg and Papen tried to secure any solution that would prevent Hitler having sole power. But after a week it became apparent that political circumstances had at last eliminated every option except the one course they wished to avoid. The hour had struck at last.

On Monday 30th January, Adolf Hitler became Chancellor of Germany. The fate of half of Europe was sealed.

An interesting group photographed in 1932 in front of a Dornier Wahl monoplane. (Left to right) Hitler's pianist, 'Putzi' Hanfstangl, Heinrich Hoffmann (for once the photographed rather than the photographer), Hitler, Schaub, Berchtoed, Baur, Bruckner, Dr Otto Dietrich, and Snyder.

Left: The original caption says that this is a photograph of the 'Day of Youth in Nuremberg' at the September Rally in 1934. Hitler spoke to 60,000 Hitler Youth in the Stadium, accompanied by Baldur von Schirach, the 'Reichsjugend-fuhrer' of the Hitler Youth. The indoctrination and rigorous physical education of the Hitler Youth movement made it an effective seed bed for the German armed forces.

Right: Hitler reviewing men of the Kriegsmarine. Hess is behind him to the left of the picture, and Admiral Raeder is behind him to the right.

Below: The Nuremberg Rally in 1937 concluded on 13th September with an inspection of members of the newly public Luftwaffe, and a display of air power – some 450 aircraft were on show at once. The new Luftwaffe, whose creation was specifically forbidden under the Treaty of Versailles, was secretly instigated as early as 1921, when pilots and engineers were trained in Russia.

Chancellor.

itler began his Chancellorship by seeking to create a working majority in the Reichstag by coalition with the Conservatives, for majority was a condition of Chancellorship laid down by Hindenburg. However, although the Cabinet had only three Nazi members in a total of eleven, Goering was appointed Minister of the Prussian interior, a post which gave him control of the police. Within hours of being in government, Hitler and Goering had, while outwardly behaving constitutionally and in accordance with the President's wishes, set in motion events which were within months to Nazify Germany and make Hitler dictator. Goering used his position to remove hundreds of republican officials and replace them with Nazis, principally drawn from the hard men of the SA and SS officer corps. An 'auxiliary force' of 50,000 men drawn from the SA, the SS and the *Stahlhelm* was formed, and became the effective police force, ruthlessly gunning down anyone who opposed Hitler and Nazi policy.

On February 24th 1933, Goering's men raided the Communist headquarters, impounded Communist literature and proclaimed that this 'proved' that the Communists were planning a revolution. On the evening of the 27th, a fire started at the Reichstag. The Nazi leadership went hotfoot to the scene, and proclaimed it instantly as a Communist crime and the start of a Communist revolution against the new government. The next day, Hitler prevailed upon Hindenburg to sign a decree 'for the protection of the people and the State' suspending constitutional liberty. Over four thousand Communist officials and party members were arrested, the Communist press and political meetings were suppressed, the Social Democratic press and organisations were proscribed. Only the Nazi and Nationalist parties were left untouched.

In fact, of course, the fire was started by a group of SA men operating under Goering's orders. Apparently coincidentally, a half-mad Dutch Communist called Marinus Van der Lubbe

The interior of the Reichstag after the fire that destroyed it in February 1933.

Below: *The Dutchman accused of starting the Reichstag fire, Marinus van der Lubbe, required an interpreter at his trial in Leipzig. Here the interpreter, in the foreground with his hand raised, is being sworn in.*

chose to set his own fires in the Reichstag that night, which gave the Nazis the opportunity to present him as the scapegoat and the proof of a Communist plot. Whatever the detailed truth of the Reichstag fire, which will never be known, it marked the end of freedom in Germany, and the beginning of tyranny.

Little more than a week later, yet another general election showed that the German people had not yet lost their reason. A majority still voted against Hitler, whose party secured 44% of the vote. But, with the Nationalists, Hitler could command a majority of the Reichstag (albeit in its temporary quarters in the Kroll Opera House), and was able to continue on his path to Germany's ruin. For that election was the last Germany was to experience until Hitler was overtaken by defeat and death.

What Hitler needed now was a two thirds majority of the Reichstag. With that he could carry out his final step to absolute power. So a plan was contrived. An enabling act would be passed by the Reichstag which would turn over the power of parliament exclusively to Hitler's cabinet for four years. To secure the necessary majority, Goering arranged to detain sufficient of the Communist and Social Democratic members of the parliament to ensure that the figures came out right. From March 23rd 1933 onwards, Germany had but one voice of government – Adolf Hitler. He always claimed thereafter, and with only a hint of a lie, that his position as dictator had been achieved legally and within the constitution. That he was so almost right in so saying must be a condemnation of the German people who allowed so flagrant a twisting of the law to go unhindered.

An informal picture of the Cabinet appointed by Hitler after his appointment as Chancellor in January 1933. Goering and Franz von Papen, now Vice Chancellor, are at his left and right. The standing figures are, starting third from left and going right, Graf Schwerin von Krosigk, Dr Wilhelm Frick, von Blomberg and Hugenberg.

Dictatorship. ▬▬▬

Within weeks, Reich Commissars turned out the governments of the ancient German States. All the State Diets were dissolved, and the Commissars were ordered to re-establish them on the basis of the last Reichstag election, with the exception that Communist seats were not to be filled. On April 7th Reich Governors were appointed to enact the policies of the Reich government. In a fortnight, Hitler had created more power in Germany than anyone else had ever had before.

The vital task of building Germany's economy was entrusted to Dr Schacht, a former head of the Reichsbank. Hitler had no knowledge or understanding of economics, and trusted Schacht implicitly to create the wealth upon which his war machine would feed. Hitler now turned, for the first time in his career, to construction rather than destruction, to evolution rather than revolution, to pacifying the forces of discontent rather than stirring them. He needed time; had no use for further disorder unless it served a particular political objective or silenced an opponent. The SA, still seeing itself as a military rather than a political force, wanted to sweep away all vestiges of the former civil and military power and rule in their stead. Hitler wanted none of it; to him the SA had been a means of forcing his way to power, a political instrument. Now that he had that power, he no longer needed the instrument. Moreover, the Army's loyalty would be very important when Hindenburg, now very old and ill, died, leaving a vacuum that he, Hitler, intended to fill. He could not afford to have the SA muddy the water with the Army. Roehm's future was clearly less than secure, although Hitler did appease him, and buy time, by making him a member of the Cabinet in December 1933.

Nor was Hitler unaware of the vulnerability of his fledgling dictatorship to outside interference. It would have been easy for France or Britain to have acted under the Treaty of Versailles to overthrow his power state, but he gambled successfully on the weakness and pacifism of other governments, and spoke loudly and frequently of peace and his wish to lead Germany away from strife. Events were soon to demonstrate just how empty such talk was. In April 1934, it became apparent that Hindenburg's health was worsening. Hitler proposed a deal with the Army – he would reduce the power and size of the SA in return for their support of his bid for the Presidency. Thus was Roehm's fate finally sealed. Himmler had, on April 1st, been detached from Roehm's command by Goering, and became head of the Prussian Gestapo. Goering was now a General of Infantry, which provided him with a much more attractive uniform. He was no longer seen in public in SA brown, and Roehm could no longer count on support from that quarter. By June, Hitler had ordered all members of the SA to take leave for the whole of July and not to wear uniform. In the last week of the month, the dying President issued an ultimatum to Hitler – restore order and the rule of law, or power would be turned over to the Army. Knowing that Hindenburg still had the power to carry out this threat, Hitler was once more near to desperation.

Near right: On the 11th September 1938, it was once again Youth Day at the annual Nuremberg Rally. Thousands of Hitler Youth saluted Hitler as he drove slowly by.

Far right: A characteristic gesture from Hitler, showing strain as war approached.

61

An early shot of the Hitler Youth, showing how much less militarised and smart they were in 1933. These lads gathered to cheer Hitler and President Hindenburg as they drove through the streets of Berlin on May Day 1933.

Right: As war approached, the Hitler Youth assumed ever-greater importance to Hitler's plans for the mightiest army the world had yet seen, and he attended many Hitler Youth rallies. Here he is reviewing Hitler Youth at the Berlin Sports Stadium with the ever-present and enigmatic Rudolf Hess (behind him on his right) and Baldur von Schirach, Reichsjugendfuehrer (Reich Youth Leader) 1933-40, almost hidden behind his shoulder. Von Schirach was Gauleiter of Vienna 1940-45.

Below: Hitler and Hess at a Nazi Party meeting in the thirties. The extent to which Hess, on the face of it a 'yes-man,' influenced Hitler's thinking has been the subject of considerable speculation.

Hitler, if in nought else, had excellent taste in cars – note the magnificent external exhaust system of this Mercedes! In this picture Hitler was taking the salute at a prewar party march-past in Weimar, but looked curiously troubled. Hess seems unusually watchful – perhaps they were expecting problems.

Above: An undated picture probably taken in September 1938. Reichsmarshall Goering, by now into his period of ever more fancy comic opera uniforms, greets Hitler on his arrival at Congress Hall during the Nuremberg Party Congress. Far right is Foreign Minister Ribbentrop, next right is Julius Streicher, Gauleiter of Franconia.

Right: Hitler and Goering at the opera – a fairly frequent occurrence in their social calendar. The programme in Goering's hand is for a performance of 'William Tell.'

Far right: This study of Hitler and Goering is from Goering's personal collection of photographs, which was sold at Christie's in London in 1973.

A photograph which somehow sums up the remarkably individual style and pageantry that Speer and Goebbels together gave the Nuremberg Rallies. Hitler addresses the faithful at the first rally after his coming to power in 1933.

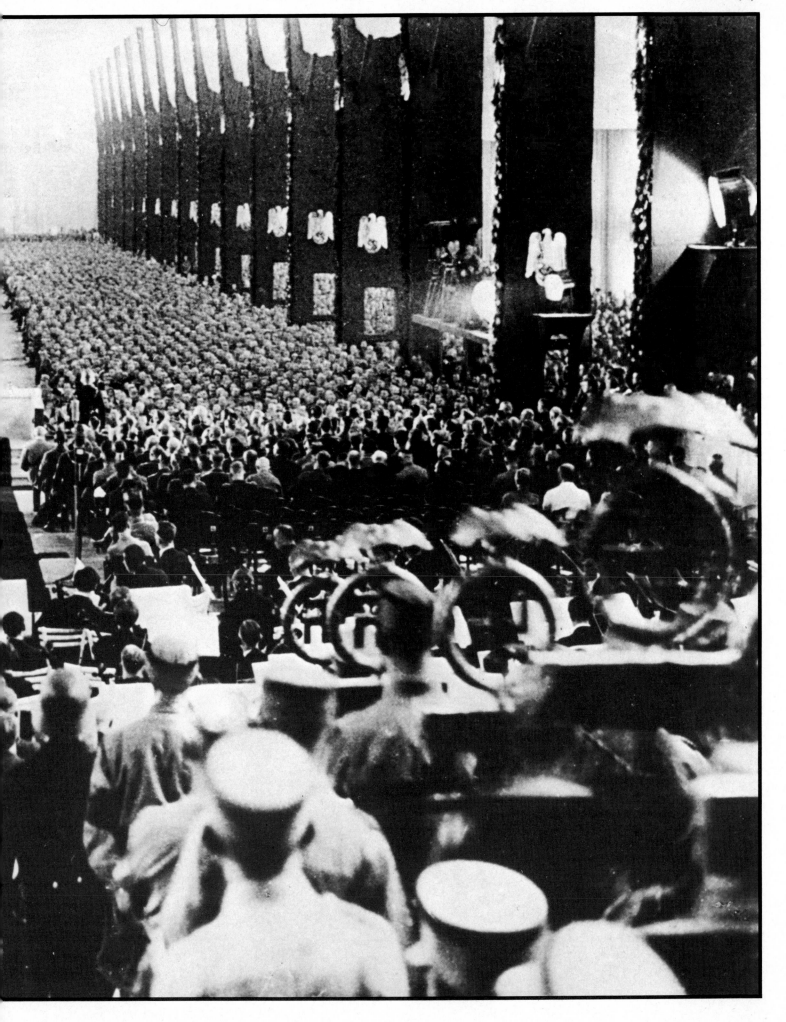

Above: *A picture dating from November 2nd 1938. Hitler and Dr Goebbels stand to applaud at a Berlin concert either side of Edda Goebbels, who in 1945 was poisoned with her children in the Berlin bunker.*

Left and top right: *In October 1937, the exiled Duke of Windsor, less than a year after his abdication from the throne as King Edward VIII, visited Germany with the Duchess and met Adolf Hitler. The meeting caused more than one storm. Dr Goebbels' propaganda machine gleefully described the Duke and Duchess, whose intentions were entirely peaceful, as "The real King and the real Queen of England," and thereby justified in the eyes of gullible Germans some of Nazism's excesses against Britain. In 1962, released German documents quoting the Duke of Coburg were widely reported in the press, suggesting that the Duke of Windsor had once favoured a British alliance with the Nazis.*

Right: *Left to right; Reichsminister Dr Josef Goebbels, Hitler and Marshal von Blomberg patronise a concert by the London Philharmonic in Berlin in November 1936.*

Purging the past.

Faced with an absolute need to show that he was able to control the SA, and that Roehm could be brought to heel, Hitler reflected on the considerable danger of the whole situation slipping out of control. In the preceding fifteen months since the Enabling Act of March 1933, the Nazi Government had 'co-ordinated' the Reich with considerable success. Conservatives, socialists and moderates had been ousted from virtually every organisation and replaced by Nazi sympathisers. There had been a continuous clamour for 'jobs for the boys', and most of those party workers who were remotely worthy, and many who were quite unworthy, had been awarded posts. Germany was now largely controlled by social misfits, incompetents, cranks and sadists – and because most of these administrators could not in fact administer without guidance and control, the true power lay more than ever before with the central government.

Only Roehm and the SA remained beyond Hitler's total control. With between three and four million men under arms, the SA was twenty to thirty times the size of the regular army. Early in 1934, Roehm had used his new Cabinet rank to propose in Cabinet that the SA should absorb the army, and that one Minister (Roehm) should control all the armed forces. This had aroused General Staff anger, and Hindenburg had been obliged to step in. As early as February 1934, Britain's Anthony Eden had expressed concern about the might of the SA in the light of the Versailles Treaty limitations. Now Hitler was being asked by Hindenburg to control at a stroke what he had been unable to control for years, with the threat of Army takeover and loss of his chances of the Presidency if he failed. He had little choice but to suppress the SA.

With all this in mind, Hitler approached a meeting with the leadership of the SA that had been arranged for some months and

Before the axe fell – Captain Ernst Roehm and the leaders of the Sturmabteilung.

Hitler's excuse for this carnage was that Roehm had been plotting against the Reich government, and his remarkable callousness was shown by his ability on that same Sunday afternoon to host a polite tea party in the gardens of the Chancellery.

Incredibly, Hindenburg and the High Command congratulated Hitler and expressed their pleasure at his resolution of the problem. Only General von Hammerstein and Field Marshal von Mackensen protested. Thus did the Army sacrifice its honour, and its ability to condemn Hitler's subsequent atrocities. It did so because it thought the decimation and humiliation of the SA leadership would bring about the end of the supremacy of Nazi private armies. But the SA lived through it, albeit with much reduced effectiveness. And, more to the point, the Army had not considered the SS, which, under Heinrich Himmler, was an infinitely more alarming enemy because it was clever as well as ruthless.

Above: Ernst Roehm when he became a Cabinet Minister at the end of 1933.

was scheduled to take place over the weekend of June 30th/July 1st at a hotel on the shores of the Tegernsee, fifty miles from Munich. In the small hours of June 30th, Roehm and Heines were tumbled out of bed. Heines and his young male bedfellow were taken outside and shot. Roehm was taken to a familiar prison in Munich and, after refusing the opportunity to shoot himself, was also shot dead.

All over Germany hundreds of other SA officers were seized and murdered. But it was not just the SA that felt the effect of Hitler's wrath. On the principle of being hung for a sheep, he took the opportunity to dispense with other troublesome opponents too. General von Schleicher and his wife were murdered at their home for complicity with Roehm. General von Bredow, a friend of Schleicher, and Gregor Strasser were shot. Erich Klausener, leader of Catholic Action was shot. Gustav von Kahr, who had ratted on the beerhall putsch, was found hacked to death. Even Father Stempfle, the editor of *Mein Kampf* died in the great purge.

Above left: Dr Hjalmar Schacht, President of the Reichsbank and Hitler's Minister of Economics from 1933 until he was dismissed for financial prudence in 1937. Schacht had been appointed in November 1923 Special Commissioner to restore the German currency after runaway inflation. By summer 1924 he had succeeded.

The death of Hindenburg.

o Hitler, the time that Hindenburg took to die must have seemed an eternity. The frail old man was all that stood between Hitler and ultimate power. Finally, after a summer of reports that he was about to die, his death came on August 2nd 1934. Just three hours later, it was announced that the offices of President and Chancellor had been combined and that Adolf Hitler had become Head of State and Commander in Chief of the Armed Forces, as well as Chancellor. The office of President was abolished. Hitler was to be known as Fuehrer and Reich Chancellor. As the ulimate act of arrogance, Hitler demanded of the armed forces a sworn oath of allegiance – not to Germany, but to him personally. No officer was excluded. The Generals were at last under control, and had lost their chance of overturning Hitler's dictatorship.

In a plebiscite on August 19th, more than thirty-eight million Germans voted their approval of Hitler's usurping the Presidency, an act specifically excluded by the Enabling Act of March 1933, which was the 'legal' basis for Hitler's dictatorship. On September 4th, Hitler heard amid the theatricality, the pageantry, the splendour and the Nazi salutes at the Party Congress in Nuremberg the Gauleiter of Bavaria proclaim that "The German form of life is definitely determined for the next thousand years." At forty-five, he was at the height of his power and of his abilities. He had mobilised in Germany a national belief in German superiority; a will to conquer and succeed at any cost. Amazingly, contemporary reports by outsiders suggest that few Germans (other than persecuted minority groups) seemed to mind the massive infringements of their civil liberties. The mass of the people genuinely set the State above all.

In a sense this was not surprising. The period from 1934 to 1938 was characterised by massive industrial rebuilding, an armaments drive such as the world had never before seen, the virtual elimination by 1936 of unemployment, and the unilateral casting off of the shackles of Versailles. Hitler used his strength at home to test his strength abroad. A Non-Aggression Pact with Poland in January 1934 had provided him with assurance that Poland would not support France if France were attacked. In March 1935, he restored conscription and began the mighty expansion of the army that was to lead to war: in the same month he allowed Goering to announce the formation of the Luftwaffe (which had actually been covertly created some two years before) in direct contravention of the Treaty of Versailles. Two months before, in a genuinely free plebiscite, the Saar, separated from Germany in 1919, voted overwhelmingly (more than 90% were in favour) to return to Germany, despite the freely reported dictatorship, tyranny, and lack of democratic freedoms. To Hitler,

President Hindenburg, who fought long for democracy in Germany, shortly before his death on 2nd August 1934.

this was proof that the attraction of German Nationalism would bring unresistingly into his fold those other Germans in Austria, Poland and Czechoslovakia.

But what of Mussolini, fascist dictator of Italy? In *Mein Kampf*, Hitler had said that Italy was the pre-destined ally against France. Mussolini, in turn, regarded Austria as the buffer between Italy and the rest of Europe, and therefore had a vested interest in Austria's independence. Hitler and Mussolini met in Venice on 14th June 1934, and Hitler renounced any desire to annexe Austria. On 25th July 1934, just after the purge of the SA in Germany, Austrian Nazis, apparently anxious to make their mark, occupied the Vienna Chancellery and murdered Dollfuss, the Austrian Chancellor. In the light of his recent pronouncements, while delighted at Dollfuss's demise, Hitler could do little else but watch as Italy installed and protected Schuschnigg as Chancellor. This humiliation did not appeal to Hitler; he watched in some alarm as Mussolini courted France.

Mussolini's war of conquest in Abyssinia produced results more to Hitler's liking. The slightly crazy undertaking which had begun in October 1935 after months of wrangling in and around the League of Nations over Italian designs in Africa ended in

Above: President Hindenburg arriving in East Prussia for a 1933 visit. Behind him are General von Blomberg, Vice-Chancellor von Papen, Goering and Koch, the President of Prussia.

Below: Hitler, Hindenburg and Goering during the Tannenberg Memorial Parade commemorating the President's great 1914 victory over the Russians

Italian victory in May 1936 with the exile of Emperor Haile Selassie and Mussolini proclaiming a new Roman Empire. But at the end of the previous year, Britain's new Foreign Secretary, Hoare (there had been a General Election in November 1935 which brought Baldwin to power) had conceived a plan for settling the Abyssinian question by partition. This had been put in secret to Laval in Paris, who had approved it. The next step was to get League of Nations approval, and imposition of the plan on Abyssinia, a member of the League. But, in some mysterious way probably known best to Pierre Laval, the plan was leaked in the French press, and it became apparent that the premier members of the League were conspiring to usurp its power.

The aged President, speaking at what should have been a political state occasion, found himself, during 1933, increasingly hemmed in by Nazi uniforms and regalia.

The occupation of the Rhineland.

Goebbels rarely missed an opportunity for cheap coverage –after the successful occupation of the Rhineland, he and Hitler were pictured with adoring 'girls from the Rhineland.'

This was music to the ears of Adolf Hitler, for the League of Nations represented the greatest single barrier to his territorial ambitions in Europe. With the premature publication of the Hoare/Laval plan, the League began to fall apart. On 27th February 1936, the 'threat' of the Franco-Soviet pact gave Hitler the excuse he needed to try one of the greatest bluffs of his career and test the resolve of his potential enemies. The German mass army was in an early stage of training and development. The experienced soldiers of the old Reichswehr were dispersed as instructors among the new regiments in training. Weapons were in short supply. The new Wehrmacht was in no shape for war. And yet, on March 7th 1936, unmoveably confident that neither Britain nor France was psychologically capable of resistance, Hitler's army occupied the demilitarised Rhineland and proved once and for all that the Treaty of Versailles was dead, and that the League of Nations was toothless.

The French government was in the run up to a General Election, recognised that resistance to Germany would require general mobilisation, and decided to hide behind the Locarno Pact which permitted military action only in the case of "flagrant aggression." Since the Rhineland was on the other side of the Maginot Line, France's mediaeval fortification that was to prove

so useless in 1940, the aggression was not considered "flagrant." The Franco-Polish pact was no help unless France was actually invaded – which it had not been, and clearly would not immediately be. In Britain, Baldwin said that British public opinion felt that Germany had done little more than liberate her own territory, and that the government could not act against such opinion. In the event, nothing was done, and Hitler was left with 300,000 troops of his fast-growing army which now numbered over a million, ensconced in the Rhineland without a shot being fired. His self-confidence, and his belief in the weakness of Britain and France, was boosted enormously. Now there was to be no stopping the ex-tramp and corporal from conquering Europe. Alone among politicians, Winston Churchill begged the world to recognise the danger, but those who believed that peace should be bargained for but never won turned deaf ears.

There can be little doubt that, if the plentiful reason for armed action against Hitler after his Rhineland invasion had been acted upon, the course of history would have been quite different. It is arguable that on Britain's and France's weakness in 1936 should be pinned responsibility for the present-day fate of Eastern Europe, and a large part of the blame for the threat to present day peace posed by the Soviet Union.

Hitler presented the occupation in the Reichstag as an act of restoration of German honour – the counterpart to the shame of Versailles. He excused Germany's violation of the Locarno Pact by stating that the Franco-Soviet Pact had broken it a month before. Beneath the bluff, General Blomberg, in command of Germany's small force, had already given the order to retreat back across the Rhine if the French made the slightest move to oppose the invasion. How different history would have been if they had.

A plebiscite of the German people on the invasion returned a 98.8% vote in favour. The German people were passionately behind Hitler. France's allies in Eastern Europe – Russia, Poland, Yugoslavia and Roumania – now saw that their pacts with France were worthless. Where would Hitler's interest alight next?

Right: General von Blomberg had advised strongly against the military occupation of the Rhineland in March 1936. On 10th April, Hitler was able to march ahead of him and other military leaders at the launching of Germany's first warship since the Great War, confident of the weakness of Britain and France. The building of the battle-cruisers Scharnhorst *and* Gneisenau *had begun secretly in 1934, in defiance of the Treaty of Versailles.*

Below: On the third anniversary of his becoming Chancellor, Hitler and Victor Lutze, Head of the SA 1934-43, review a parade of the Old Guard in the Berlin Lustgarten.

Hitler arrives at the British Embassy in Berlin on 28th March 1935 for lunch with Sir John Simon and Mr Anthony Eden during prolonged Anglo-German talks.

Above: *Hitler arriving at the Berlin Olympics in 1936, surrounded by members of the Olympic Committee.*

Right: *Nazi salutes from German winner (European Champion Sietas) and runner-up P. Schwarz after an Olympic swimming event. Denmark's H. Malstroem is not impressed.*

Far right: *The Olympic torch, carried 1,800 miles by 3,000 runners through seven countries, lights the Olympic flame in the Berlin Lustgarten in 1936.*

Below: *The Olympic stadium was put to maximum political use. Here Hitler is greeted as he arrives to make his 1936 May Day speech.*

The Spanish Civil War.

This picture was filed on 4th August 1936. It shows Government (Left wing) troops firing on Franco's fascist rebels in San Sebastian.

Two and a half months after the victorious end of Mussolini's African adventure in Abyssinia, Hitler received on July 22nd at Bayreuth, after an evening of his beloved Wagner, a letter from General Franco. A week earlier, the Spanish fascist had staged a military revolt in Spain, and civil war had broken out. Goering and Blomberg happened also to be in Bayreuth, and a hasty conference was convened. Without conferring with others of his colleagues, Adolf Hitler made another of his inspired political decisions that was to do so much to reshape the world to its disadvantage. Germany was to aid Franco in his fight against the Left.

The Nazi regime supplied aircraft, tanks, technicians, and money to the tune of half a billion marks. The emergent Luftwaffe also made available an entire unit – known as the Condor Legion – which wrought the first major atrocity by the Thousand Year Reich outside its own boundaries when it destroyed the town of Guernica and most of its civilian inhabitants. The reasons for Hitler's desire to do so much in Spain are not as obvious as they at first seem. Certainly, he was opposing the hated Bolshevism, but Hitler himself admitted that his objective in Spain was not to bring about an end of the war, but to prolong it and thereby maintain a state of tension in the Mediterranean which would bring Italy and Mussolini into his pocket. For Mussolini was committed to aiding Franco to a far greater degree than Hitler, and Italy fielded between sixty and seventy thousand troops in support of Franco's objectives. While the West disapproved of the war, and while the war continued, Mussolini was disaffected from France and Britain. On November 5th 1937 Hitler actually said to his generals and his Foreign Minister that "a hundred per cent victory for Franco" was "not desirable from the German point of view."

A further major benefit to Germany arising from the Civil War was the opportunity to prove its weapons and train its airmen in active service conditions. The Luftwaffe perfected in Spain the dive bombing techniques of the Stukas and the heavy bombing of civilian areas that were later used so devastatingly in the *Blitzkrieg* attacks elsewhere in Europe. After the Civil War, Germany had a corps of battle trained airmen that no other nation in the world (with the possible exception of Japan) possessed – an invaluable asset in the training of new pilots.

The war succeeded in its objective for Hitler of keeping Italy and the Western democracies in a state of perpetual disagreement. From that disagreement came the Berlin-Rome axis, about which the Second World War was to pivot. On October 21st 1936, Mussolini's son-in-law, Count Ciano, signed in Berlin, after a visit to Hitler in Berchtesgaden, a protocol that set out a common policy for Germany and Italy in foreign affairs. In November, this was followed by Ribbentrop's Anti-Comintern Pact with Japan. A secret protocol within this pact provided for Germany and Japan making no treaties with Soviet Russia without the other's consent, and for mutual assistance in the event of Russian attack. It was essentially a propaganda exercise, but it laid a further foundation for future events.

Men of the mighty Italian Legion in Spain march past General Franco before assembled Italian aircraft.
Mussolini's commitment to Franco's cause was very great.

Described in the original caption as 'the first authenticated pictures (not posed) of the Civil War in Spain', and dated 24th July 1936, this picture shows Franco rebels firing over their dead horses in Madrid.

A shot dated 20th November 1936 showing Government troops defending a suburban street in Madrid behind a barricade of sandbags and bricks.

As Franco pressed home the Republican attack on the capital, the men of the communist International Brigade move forward to fight for the Government.

Government soldiers of the Navarra regiment resting in a square after capturing Tarragona on their way to Barcelona.

The decision that war would come. ▀▀▀▀▀▀

A fine study of Britain's premier Neville Chamberlain in earnest conversation with Benito Mussolini at the Munich Conference in September 1938.

With hindsight it seems incredible that the great mass of the German people did not realise that Hitler's objectives were to be achieved by war. In his first four years, reviewed in a speech made to the Reichstag on 30th January 1937, Hitler's government had eradicated unemployment, reasserted German self-esteem, created massive industrial production, raised the standard of living in Germany immeasurably, and built up a powerful Navy, Army and Air Force. By contrast with the poor economies, endless flabby compromises and lacklustre policies of the other Western powers, Germany had direction, guts, a future. Germans were proud to be German. But right up to September 1939, most ordinary Germans believed – with good reason in the light of successive crises during which Germany's opponents simply gave in – that Hitler would always get his way without bloodshed. Such was the magic of the man and his oratory that Germans found it difficult to understand that other nations found their miracle less attractive than they did.

Yet, in 1936, Goering had been put in charge of a Four Year Plan whose objective was preparation for war. At the end of 1936, in a speech to industrialists, Goering said that "No limit on rearmament can be visualised. The only alternatives are victory or destruction. We live in a time when the final battle is in sight."

During the first half of 1937, Hitler devoted much time to further courtship of Italy, and to hardening up the Berlin-Rome Axis. Mussolini finally agreed to visit Germany for the first time in September, and was feted in grand style, returning to Rome convinced that the only future for Italy was at the side of the Fuehrer. On November 6th, Ribbentrop went to Rome to secure Mussolini's signature on the Anti-Comintern Pact, and Mussolini intimated that he no longer stood between Hitler and Austria. Also in November 1937, on the 19th, occurred Hitler's first meeting with Lord Halifax, Foreign Secretary under Britain's new Prime Minister, Neville Chamberlain. Halifax went to Berchtesgaden, armed with a brief from Chamberlain to sound out the possibility of an understanding with Germany. The German memorandum that summarised the conversation indicates that Chamberlain was prepared to trade a general settlement of affairs in Western Europe for concessions to Hitler regarding colonies and Eastern Europe.

What Chamberlain and Halifax did not know was that just two weeks before that encounter, on November 5th, a meeting at the Wilhelmstrasse of Hitler, his Foreign Minister von Neurath and his service chiefs – Goering, Admiral Raeder, Field Marshal Blomberg, and Colonel General Baron von Fritsch – made the most fateful decision any committee of the Third Reich ever

and the Czech Sudetenland were set for 1938 and, to their horrified amazement, the armed forces were warned to be ready to go to war with Britain and France if necessary. Their horror was due simply to the fact that the build-up of the three services still had a long way to go before they were ready to take on a war with any expectation of winning it. Blomberg, Fritsch and Neurath doubted that the decision to embark on conquest was yet wise, and had the temerity to say so. All three were out of office by the

One wonders whether, at wartime planning sessions at the map table like this one in 1941, Hitler regretted that famous decision of November 1937 that war would come. On either side of Hitler are (left) General Walther von Brauchitsch and (right) General Halder.

made. They decided on the basis of a memorandum prepared by Blomberg that Germany "had a right to greater living space *(lebensraum)* than other peoples" and that "Germany's future was wholly conditional upon the solving of the need for space."

Thus was born the *lebensraum* policy. At the same meeting, Hitler decreed that "Germany's problem could be solved only by means of force." The meeting considered a number of hypothetical political situations in Europe which might be expected to precipitate war, and determined how it would take advantage of each. The deadline for conquest was set as not later than 1943-5. The annexations of Czechoslovakia and Austria in the near future were discussed in detail – Hitler believed that Britain and France had already tacitly written off Czechoslovakia, and that Britain would not go to war with Germany under any forseeable circumstances because of difficulties with her Empire. He also said that he did not believe that Russia would interfere because of the commitment from Japan.

From that meeting in the Wilhelmstrasse emerged the final decision that Germany would go to war. As yet, no date was set for the major confrontation, although the annexations of Austria

New Year, Neurath after several heart attacks brought on by the worry of having all semblance of coherent foreign policy snatched from him.

Suddenly, the wily, often inspired and always politically shrewd Hitler had begun to make decisions that had little basis in sound common sense. For the first time, his closest associates began to believe that he might be deluding himself as to what could be attained. In the years to follow, the trait of total unwillingness to accept criticism, and naked fury at dissension with his ideas that had always been part of Hitler's character became more dominant, more frequently a part of decision making. From 1938 onwards, Hitler's decisions became progressively worse, his determination to be sole arbiter of policy steadily greater. Some investigators have sought evidence of a change of mental state at about this time, although none has produced clear indications of the onset of any imbalance that was not already there. Nonetheless, it is indisputable that 1937/1938 marked the beginning not only of Germany's commitment to war, but also of Hitler's tendency to megalomaniacal mismanagement of affairs both military and civil.

Britain's Prime Minister Neville Chamberlain and German Foreign Minister Joachim von Ribbentrop flanked by SS and military uniforms during the Czech crisis in 1938.

Above: Benito Mussolini in Berlin during his first ceremonial visit to Germany in 1937.

Below: In March 1939, Hitler visited Italy to confer with Il Duce. This picture was taken in Florence. The ubiquitous Rudolf Hess is in the background on the right.

Right: An impressive display of the German-Italian solidarity that Hitler struggled so hard to promote as Mussolini and Hitler meet with their respective Foreign Ministers in Berlin. In front are (left to right) Goering, Mussolini, Hitler and Count Ciano. Between Ciano and Hitler can be seen SS chief Heinrich Himmler.

Mussolini and Hitler, in a Mercedes driven by an SS officer, pass black-uniformed SS troops during Mussolini's whirlwind visit to Germany in 1937.

Hitler and Goering shake hands – a propaganda picture released on 25th February 1939 to promote 'Luftwaffe Day,' which took place on March 1st. On Luftwaffe Day, after the inevitable parades and speeches, Goering decorated successful officers in the ceremonial room of his Air Ministry.

Mussolini, overwhelmed by the sheer power displayed by Hitler during the 1937 visit, takes the salute at one of the many military parades arranged for him.

Above left: *An anxious Mussolini flies in for the 1942 Berchtesgaden conference to plan 'Hercules', the attack on Malta. Between Hitler and Mussolini can be seen Field Marshal Albert Kesselring. On Hitler's left is General Wilhelm Keitel.*

Above right: *Five years earlier, Mussolini was more relaxed, during his 1937 visit to Germany.*

Above: *The sheer style of Hitler's pageantry, processions and military parades during Mussolini's visit in 1937 left an indelible impression upon the Italian dictator. This Berlin motorcade of the best that Mercedes could sell has just passed through the Brandenburg gate, now part of the boundary between East and West Berlin. Mussolini did his best to equal the effect when Hitler visited Italy but never quite succeeded.*

Left: *When Hitler visited Rome in May 1938, Mussolini was being wooed to the cause of war. Here they arrive at Massenzio Hall, Rome. Ribbentrop, wary as ever, is between the dictators. Hess is behind Mussolini.*

Right: *Bemused by the apparently endless uniforms and salutes, Mussolini walks with Hitler during the 1937 visit.*

Hitler surrounded by children and officers of the SS and Wehrmacht in Berlin on 15th June 1938 after 'starting the work of the reconstruction of Berlin.' This pet project, for which Albert Speer was his architect, was to make the city "the most beautiful in the world."

Far left: On Hitler's 50th birthday, 20th April 1939, Heinrich Hoffmann, his photographer, shot this picture of Hitler 'with the children of his ministers.' Hitler was in fact never fond of children, and this photograph was a propaganda exercise to endow Hitler with qualities beloved by the German people. It is interesting to reflect that Goebbels' children were callously poisoned in the Berlin bunker as the Russians approached in 1945.

Above: This propaganda picture issued by Dr Goebbels' Propaganda Ministry in March 1939 was claimed to show joyful Nazi sympathisers watching the entry of German troops into Brno during the Czech invasion. The caption went on to state that 'this is the furthest point eastward to be reached by the invaders and . . . Hitler will review his conquering army there.' The shot could in fact have been taken in any German town.

Left: An earlier 1937 propaganda picture of Hitler shaking hands with a 'traditionally dressed peasant girl during a visit to Buckeberg in 1937.' Such pictures were artfully stage managed by the propagandists to enhance the public's impression of Hitler's almost non-existent closeness to the people.

This news picture taken during a visit to Berlin by Mussolini and his son-in-law Count Ciano shows (right to left) Mussolini, Hitler, Count Ciano, Goering and Himmler with other senior German and Italian officers.

Franco was justifiably wary of committing Spain to Germany's war. After this meeting in the Franco-Spanish border town of Hendaye on 23rd October 1940, during which Franco evaded all commitment, Hitler said to Mussolini "Rather than go through that again, I would prefer to have three or four teeth yanked out."

Compare the sombre expressions at the above meeting of Mussolini, Hitler and Ciano in a train at the Brenner Pass on October 5th 1940 with the smiles in the streets of Florence two and a half years earlier.

The end of Austria.

In February, Dr Kurt von Schuschnigg, Chancellor of Austria, was invited to meet Hitler at Berchtesgaden, and was subjected to a two hour ranting tirade of abuse against Austria and its present and past failings in the eyes of Germany as represented by Hitler. Later the same day, Schuschnigg was presented with a document to sign. This was in effect an agreement to cede Austria to Germany, failing which Germany would conquer Austria by force. Schuschnigg, under heavy pressure from Papen and Hitler, agreed to sign, but secured four days grace during which to confer with President Miklas and produce a 'binding agreement.' Not surprisingly, Miklas objected. Hitler responded by having Keitel spread news of entirely bogus military operations apparently aimed at Austria. Over the next two weeks Hitler broadcast to the Austrians, Schuschnigg spoke in the Austrian Parliament against annexation, and, on March 9th, announced that there would on March 13th be a plebiscite of the Austrian people – 'yes' or 'no' to

Hitler's triumphal arrival in Vienna on Monday March 14th 1938 after the Anschluss was an occasion for delirious excitement, as it had been three days earlier when he had arrived in Linz, where he had gone to school. **Above:** *Hitler shakes the hand of an old lady in the crowd.*

Right: *The victory parade through the streets of Vienna.*

Germany. Hitler went into a fury, called Goering, and ordered the Generals to prepare to invade two days later, on Saturday the 12th of March.

On March 11th, Hitler demanded that the plebiscite be called off, which, surprisingly, Schuschnigg agreed to do. So Hitler increased the stakes, demanding that Seyss-Inquart, his Nazi leader in Austria, be made Chancellor at once. President Miklas refused, Schuschnigg resigned, and still Miklas stood out against German pressure. The next day, Germany marched, and independent Austria was no more. Hitler lost no time in going to Austria that same day and received a rapturous welcome, especially in Linz, where he laid a wreath on the grave of his parents. He proclaimed that there would be a plebiscite on the *Anschluss* throughout the whole of Germany on April 10th – and Germany, as far as he was concerned, now included Austria. In that plebiscite, carried out with watchful eyes on the votes being cast, 99% voted 'yes.'

Hitler "bringing freedom" to Asch in the Sudetenland, 3rd October 1938 "to the boundless rejoicing of the entire population"

The savagery that followed in Vienna and the towns of Austria was appalling. Hundreds of Jews were arrested and humiliated. Tens of thousands were imprisoned. Before the war began just over a year later, some 180,000 Jews had bought their way out of Austria by handing over all their possessions to Heydrich's 'Office for Jewish Emigration.' This organisation, run by Adolf Eichmann, became eventually an office of extermination rather than emigration, and was directly responsible for the deaths of more than four million people snatched from the length and breadth of Hitler's 'empire.' A massive concentration camp at Mauthausen provided facilities for these appalling crimes. A total of 35,318 people were murdered at Mauthausen before the end of the war.

Hitler's army was now flanking Czechoslovakia on three sides. The stage was set for the next act.

After his triumphal visits as conqueror to Linz and Vienna – another picture of the tumultuously successful Vienna victory parade is below – Hitler returned to Berlin by air. In this picture, Hermann Goering, wearing what seems to be more than his fair share of decorations, walks beside Hitler.

Obviously an important funeral, to have turned out most of the Nazi hierarchy – but whose? There is no caption on the picture, and the author has been unable to make a clear indentification of the occasion, although it seems to have taken place in about 1934.

The Sudetenland.

Hitler greets Neville Chamberlain in September 1938 for the Munich Conference which 'resolved' the Czech crisis by the surrender of the Sudetenland.

Sf Czechoslovakia's ten million inhabitants, three and a half million were Sudeten Germans – people who spoke German, and were of German background and culture, but had never been a part of Germany itself. The Republic of Czechoslovakia had been created in 1918, with substantial built-in minorities, of which the Germans were the largest. Those Germans had taken to National Socialism with enthusiasm. Now, after the annexation of Austria, Konrad Henlein, the Sudeten Nazi leader, visited Hitler for three hours on March 28th. Hitler told Henlein simply to make demands that would be 'unacceptable to the Czech government.' Hitler wanted Czechoslovakia, and needed an excuse for the world to accept as a valid reason for his taking it.

In April and May 1938, the British and French governments, ever anxious to appease, urged President Benes to give way to the Sudeten German demands. Hitler was cynically grateful, and told Henlein to step up his requirements, and to deny when he visited London that he was acting on instructions from Berlin. By May 17th, Hitler was enquiring anxiously about German military strength and readiness on the Czech border, and seeking details of the Maginot Line-like fortifications which had been built by the Czechs.

The weekend beginning May 20th became known as the 'May Crisis.' British and Czech Intelligence believed German troops were massed on the border, and Dr Goebbels' propaganda assault was stepped up sharply. On the afternoon of the 20th,

Only six months after the Munich Conference, Germany occupied Bohemia and Moravia in defiance of the Munich agreement. Here troops enter Brno.

Benes ordered partial mobilisation. The Czechs were ready for a fight, and Hitler was furious. On the Monday, Hitler backed down, announced he had no aggressive intentions, and bided his time, while London and Paris congratulated themselves on teaching the dictator a lesson.

By May 30th, Hitler had issued a secret directive which began "It is my unalterable intention to smash Czechoslovakia by military action in the near future." The deadline was set. The attack was to be on October 1st 1938. As the summer came, Hitler found himself facing a near revolt among the General Staff, who believed that the massing of force against Czechoslovakia would result in the Western wall falling to the French, and that Germany was risking a major war it would not win to satisfy petty greed. Once again, a strong conviction was abroad that logic and rational thought had deserted the Fuehrer. General Ludwig Beck, the Chief of the General Staff, bravely fought the case, but by August 18th he had lost the battle and had been deserted by his ally General von Brauchitsch, so resigned. Hitler forbade any mention of Beck's resignation in the press, and it is possible that Britain knew nothing of it until October when it was announced in Germany. Beck was succeeded by General Halder, around whom a major conspiracy against Hitler began to develop. But the conspiracy was to be stillborn, for it rested upon the assumption that Britain would not allow the Sudetenland to be snatched without a fight.

In June, Chamberlain let it be known that Britain would not stand in the way if a plebiscite showed that a majority of the Sudeten Germans wished to be part of Germany. By early August it was clear that neither Britain nor France would intervene, but the position of Soviet Russia, co-guarantor with France of Czech independence, was unclear. When the annual Nuremberg Party Rally began in September, everybody in Germany and abroad expected an announcement of invasion. Gas masks were distributed in Prague. The tension was unbearable. Halder and the generals finalised plans to overthrow Hitler when he returned to Berlin from Nuremberg. But Hitler's Nuremberg speech merely repeated his arguments and assertions about the Sudetenland, and, to the generals' dismay, he did not return to Berlin, but instead went to Berchtesgaden to meet Neville Chamberlain.

During his meeting with Hitler, Chamberlain gave a personal assurance of non-intervention in Czechoslovakia, and again on September 22nd and 23rd, visited Berchtesgaden to try to avoid a wider conflict that would arise if the Czechs defended their territory with Russian support. In London and Paris schoolchildren were evacuated, trenches were dug, the people prepared for war. Even Goering, on the 28th September, told Jodl that "A Great War can hardly be averted any longer." Halder and the generals set their coup for the next day, September 29th. Hitler was nearer to being toppled from power than at any other time. But, unrealised by the Generals, and even less by Chamberlain and Daladier, Hitler did not want war at that stage of events. He knew Germany was not ready even for a limited confrontation with the Czechs, who had mobilised a million men, as many as Germany had for both the Eastern and the Western fronts. His objective was to take the Sudetenland without war. The question was – how?

Mussolini provided the excuse by asking Hitler, on 28th September, to refrain from mobilisation. Hitler sent a message to Chamberlain that, in the light of this request, he would see Chamberlain, Daladier and Mussolini in Munich the next day. The Czechs were not even invited to their own funeral.

The SS played a crucial role in securing Germany's psychological dominance over Europe. Compare the unmilitary appearance of Heinrich Himmler in this early picture with the military precision of the SS some five years later **(opposite)**.

Hitler takes the salute at the march past of the Black Guards on his birthday, probably in 1938.

Hess, Himmler and Hitler reviewing SS troops in the courtyard of the Deutsche Hotel, Nuremberg in 1938.

The tough but beleaguered Dr Hacha, President of Czechoslovakia, meets Hitler at Hradcany Castle, ancient seat of the kings of Bohemia in Prague.

On March 22nd 1939, Hitler and Admiral Raeder put to sea in the pocket battleship Deutschland. They sailed to take the tiny Baltic coastal district of Memel, a part of Lithuania, to which Germany had been laying claim against a background of SS infiltration of the populace for some months. The seaborne arrival was designed to provide the Navy with some credit after the successes of the army in Austria and Czechoslovakia, but the Lithuanians took their time about surrendering and Hitler got very seasick and extremely impatient. Finally, at 2.30 pm on 23rd March, Hitler made another of his triumphal entries. **Right:** The speech to the populace and the world. **Below:** Inspecting the guard of honour on landing **Below right:** Hitler left Berlin for the Memel adventure by train. Admiral Raeder is on his left.

Left: Only a week before the occupation of Memel, Hitler had made his triumphal entry into Prague at the conclusion of the latest of Germany's lightning conquests, this time in direct defiance of the Munich Agreement of a mere six months earlier. In this picture he is shown passing through Aach on his progress through Czechoslovakia, apparently cheered all the way by enthusiastic Czechs, if one is to believe the pictures released by the Propaganda Ministry.

Below: Once in Prague, Hitler saw to it that considerable armaments were displayed to demonstrate German strength both to the people of Czechoslovakia, and to the world that watched in considerable trepidation. If Chamberlain and Daladier had made in mid-1938 the stand that Chamberlain made over Poland in mid-1939, the Second World War might never have happened. If Britain and France had made swift retribution when Hitler occupied the Rhineland in 1936, it is almost certain that there would have been no war.

The Munich Agreement.

To the Conference were presented proposals ostensibly prepared by Mussolini, which were welcomed by the appeasers of Britain and France. In fact, it transpired after the war, the 'Italian' proposals had been drafted by Goering and von Neurath in Berlin, and phoned by the Italian Ambassador to Mussolini. So anxious were Chamberlain and Daladier to give Hitler all he asked and thus avoid war, that the proposals became progressively more disastrous for the Czechs as the conference wore on. When the Agreement was signed at 1 am on September 30th, it stipulated that the Czechs must evacuate the Sudetenland, and that it would be occupied by the Germans by October 10th. Britain and France had deserted the Czechs and left them to a terrible fate. The final agreement on November 20th 1938 gave Germany 11,000 square miles of their country. Czechoslovakia lost 66 per cent of its coal resources, 86 per cent of its chemicals, 70 per cent of its electric power, 70 per cent of its iron and steel. Even Poland and Hungary snatched parts of the devastated country with Ribbentrop's connivance.

As Chamberlain rushed excitedly back to Britain to wave his scrap of paper signed absent-mindedly by Hitler that morning, and proclaim "Peace in our time," he did not know that at that same meeting in Munich, Mussolini and Hitler had agreed that the time would come when they would fight side by side against Britain and France.

But for Chamberlain and Daladier's willingness to give Hitler anything, Hitler would, to save face, have attacked Czechoslovakia on October 1st. Few now doubt that the Germans would have lost the resulting war with Britain and France. Hitler's prestige and self-confidence were boosted enormously. His old political sense had not yet completely deserted him. Confidently, within days of entering the Sudetenland, he set about breaking the Munich agreement by planning the annexation of the rest of Czechoslovakia. After a winter of manoeuvre and counter manoeuvre, with the Czech government powerless without its allies, the Germans entered Bohemia and Moravia on 15th March 1939. Hitler entered Prague, proclaimed the Protectorate of Bohemia and Moravia, and took as his residence the ancient castle of the Kings of Bohemia. Slovakia followed on 16th March.

A reappraisal of *'Mein Kampf'* would have told any observer that Poland was next on Hitler's shopping list.

Above: The clash of temperaments at the Munich conference in September 1938 helped to bring about the Second World War. After experiencing the haste with which Chamberlain and Daladier abandoned any pretence of defending Czech sovereignty in their search for peace at any price, Hitler became convinced that France and Britain would never go to war. In this picture, (left to right) Neville Chamberlain clutches a piece of paper (not the famous one – he did not get that until the following day), Daladier glowers and will not look to the camera, Hitler is defiantly triumphant, Mussolini is clearly unsure who has won but is sure it is not he, and Ciano knows exactly what has happened and has no taste for it.

Right: Six months later, the German columns roll into Czechoslovakia in defiance of the agreement.

124

The rapturous reception given to Hitler on his return to Berlin from Munich on 2nd October 1938 showed recognition by the German people of the tremendous political victory that had been won.

Hand extended in the salute that typified tyranny across Europe, Adolf Hitler stares down at the columns that have subjugated Europe.

The signing of the Pact of Steel in Berlin on May 23rd 1939. Count Ciano (left), Italian Foreign Minister signs on behalf of Italy, and Hitler studiously takes no notice.

The persecution of the Jews in Germany and the occupied countries grew rapidly after 1938 to the proportions of genocide on a scale the world has never seen before or since. **Left:** Small beginnings to the persecution – a picket outside a Jewish shop in Berlin. **Right:** A picture to rend the heart. Children destined to die in one of Himmler's concentration camps. **Below:** The horrors of extermination spread to Poland and elsewhere. The Warsaw ghetto was home to 500,000 jews, few of whom survived the war.

hile the attention of the world had been held by the events of the international stage, the German people were discovering the nature of the monster it had espoused. Although public knowledge of the concentration camps was very slight at this stage, the persecution of the Jews and of all who disagreed with the Nazis was obvious and appalling to all right minded Germans. On the 'Night of the Broken Glass', November 9th/10th 1938, 119 synagogues were burned, 7,500 Jewish shops were looted, an indeterminate number of Jews were killed and raped. The insurance bill for broken glass alone came to five million marks ($1,250,000) – and the Nazis confiscated the insurance money. Over the remaining years of the Reich, the scale of the atrocities mounted until more than six million Jews had been murdered, countless dissidents had been tortured, imprisoned and killed, and whole populations of towns and villages in 'protected' territories had been wiped out – the story of Lidice is terrifying reading. Memoranda captured after the war show clearly that Hitler was personally responsible for urging these vicious acts, and for most other crimes against Jewry and racial minorities.

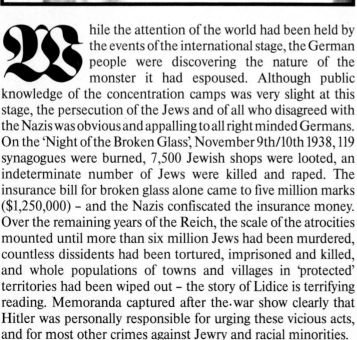

The image of this little boy in Warsaw shocked the world and became a wartime symbol of the horrors of Nazi persecution of the Jews. Amazingly he survived and is today a prosperous London businessman. He has never forgotten his ordeal in spring 1943.

Hitler making his 13th September policy speech at the 1938 Nuremberg Congress, when half Europe expected him to announce an invasion of Czechoslovakia. Instead he simply repeated his position on the Sudetenland.

Danzig, and the Pact with Russia.

The surrender to Germany of Memel, a part of Lithuania which was coveted by Stalin, emphasised to the USSR the need to play its cards carefully with Hitler. Here German Foreign Minister Ribbentrop signs the Pact on 23rd March 1939, watched by Dr Urbsys, the Lithuanian Minister.

But it was foreign policy that dominated Hitler's thoughts in 1939. Alan Bullock, in his 'Hitler – A study in tyranny,' postulated that Hitler was in the end destroyed by the same human failing that disposed of Napoleon's vaulting ambitions – an acute inability to know when to stop. By the Spring of 1939, the sheer scale of Hitler's political accomplishment was, and will probably remain, unequalled. By a combination of intuitive insight, sheer bluff and often ill-supported threats, he had coerced two of the world's greatest powers into acquiescence at his occupying and subjugating two fine nations. He had repudiated a Treaty whose very function was to prevent a rebirth of Germany's military power, and had got away with it. He had, almost legally, overthrown a constitutional Presidency and parliament and usurped their powers to himself. He had rebuilt Germany's pride, eliminated unemployment, created the world's finest army, re-established a stable currency. He was just fifty.

When on 14th April, after Italy's invasion of Albania, President Roosevelt addressed a major political speech at Hitler, asking for assurances that Germany had no further territorial ambitions in Europe, Hitler replied in the Reichstag with what was probably the finest speech he ever made, drawing parallels between his position in seeking *lebensraum* – living space – with that of the USA. He said that although the USA had only one third more inhabitants than Greater Germany, it had fifteen times the living space – and that that space had not been gained at the

conference table, but by occupation and war. He assured Roosevelt ironically that the rumours of his intended invasion of the USA were false. He made endless political points against the USA without ever answering the US President's question. Few outside the Reich were fooled by his brilliant rhetoric. But, in Germany at least, he made Roosevelt's speech a laughing stock.

After the roller coaster of events which led to the annexation of Austria, the invasion of Czechoslovakia and the occupation of Memel on the Baltic, Hitler might have been expected to take stock and do little. He had achieved so much at very little cost, with hardly a shot being fired. But his drive to conquest urged him on to take Poland, with whom negotiations had been in progress since the previous year. The Versailles Treaty had made the formerly German Danzig into a free city, and had given Germany and Poland equal rights of access. To provide Poland with access to the port, a Polish Corridor had been defined which divided East Prussia from the rest of Germany. Thus Hitler's policy of a Greater Germany provided a ready basis for dispute with the Poles and progressively greater insistence from Ribbentrop that the Poles must accept the return of Danzig to the Reich, and the creation of an extra-territorial highway linking the Reich with East Prussia. Hitler was surprised to find that the Poles, represented by Colonel Beck, their able and tough Foreign Minister, resolutely refused to consider the proposal and even, as the Spring of 1939 progressed towards Summer, made it quite clear that Poland was prepared to fight.

Vyacheslav Molotov, who became Russian Foreign Minister in May 1939, pictured in 1945.

He was even more surprised to find, at the end of March and early in April, a much changed public attitude emanating from Chamberlain and the British Government, although he doubted that Britain would put her tough words into action if pressed. On March 31st, after the events in Czechoslovakia had stunned Europe so soon after the Munich Agreement, Chamberlain announced in the House of Commons that Britain would give all the support in its power to Poland, if Polish independence were threatened. Taken at face value, this implied a threat from the West, if Germany attacked to the East. But Hitler just did not believe that the weak men over whom he had ridden roughshod in Munich would go to war for the Poles.

Hitler knew that, if he could isolate Poland from help, Polish resistance would be little for his mighty army to fear. After the Czechoslovakian experience, he saw no likelihood of either of the Western powers coming to Poland's aid, despite Chamberlain's announcement. Soviet Russia was another matter. In April, the Russian Foreign Minister, Litvinov, had put a proposal to Britain and France for a tripartite pact providing for mutual assistance backed by a military convention. Britain had virtually rejected the proposal, thereby reinforcing Hitler's view that Britain would do anything to avoid war. Only at the end of May did Chamberlain half-heartedly put counter proposals. In the meantime, Russia, in the person of Molotov, who had replaced Litvinov as Foreign Minister in May, and was much less orientated to France and Britain, was sounding out German views on a mutual non-aggression pact.

Hitler played a cool hand with Russia. Even this proposed Treaty, if it could be brought to fruition, was not sufficient security for the Fuehrer. He had long hankered after an absolute treaty of mutual assistance with Italy, which Mussolini had resisted because of his fear that Hitler would drag Italy into a war. Italy's invasion of Albania had drawn some fire away from Hitler, and the Duce was beginning to feel the diplomatic heat of Britain and France's opposition. After reassurances from Ribbentrop, which, like virtually every assurance Ribbentrop ever gave, were totally false, that Germany wanted a period of peace once the Danzig issue was settled, Mussolini was swayed into allowing Foreign Minister Count Ciano to sign the Pact of Steel in Berlin on 21st May. This committed Italy and Germany to total partnership in war and defence. Mussolini was committed to his eventual downfall, and Hitler had secured his southern boundary.

All Summer, Hitler was in Berchtesgaden, planning his invasion of Poland, provisionally set for the beginning of September. Since May, when the Russians had sounded the German view of a pact, he had been aware of the need to approach the USSR from a position of strength. He realised that Stalin wanted to avoid being drawn into war, and that the ruler of Russia also saw possibilities for territorial gains in Eastern Europe if he were to turn a blind eye, under cover of a pact of non-aggression, to Hitler's activities on Germany's eastern boundaries. Stalin had already, by withdrawing Soviet aid from the Left-wing Spanish Republicans in 1938, ensured the end of the Civil War in Franco's favour, and had thereby detached the USSR from the risk of war arising from Mediterranean involvement. Now, having just purged and liquidated most of the best officers from the Red Army, Stalin was in no position to be dragged into a fight. But it was not until the end of June that Hitler made his approach. Even then, when the Germans found the Russians tougher negotiators than the Western powers, Hitler allowed the discussions to pass into limbo for three weeks. On 18th July, the Russians took the initiative to reopen the economic talks of the previous winter. Then, at the end of July, Hitler began to put the pressure on, largely because Britain and France had made fresh overtures to the Soviet Union, and Stalin showed signs of playing a double game by negotiating with both sides at once.

In mid-August, an alarmed Count Ciano met Hitler at Berchtesgaden to plead on behalf of the Duce for avoidance of war, and left convinced that the attack on Poland was inevitable. On the 14th, Ribbentrop put the pressure on Molotov – but the Russians, having been obliged to wait for Hitler, now played hard to get. Not until Hitler appealed personally to Stalin, accepting in his message Molotov's draft of a non-aggression pact, did Russia accept that Ribbentrop should go to the USSR with full powers to sign the treaty on Germany's behalf. Ribbentrop went on August 22nd 1939.

On the 21st, the British Cabinet had met, and had decided that a pact of non-aggression between Germany and USSR would have no effect on their obligations to Poland, or on their willingness to honour those obligations. The British Ambassador in Berlin delivered personally to Hitler a note from Chamberlain reaffirming Britain's position, and was treated to an hysterical tirade recounting entirely fictitious Polish excesses against the German minority in Poland, and blaming Britain's guarantee to Poland for the state of international tension. Hitler gave the Ambassador the impression that he was a man whose reason had temporarily deserted him. And yet, as soon as the Ambassador had gone, Hitler, according to one of his ministers, laughed and said that "Chamberlain won't survive that conversation." That evening he set the date for the attack on Poland as Saturday 26th August.

The pact with Russia was signed on the 24th – Churchill described it as 'such an unnatural act.' On the same day, the British Parliament united with Chamberlain in its determination to stand behind Poland. Hitler became worried, and decided to try just one more time to isolate Poland from her Western allies. In a totally different meeting with Henderson, the British Ambassador, he sought reconciliation with Britain, without retreating one jot from his intention to attack Poland – he tried in fact to re-create the scenario of the Czech crisis of 1938. Grandly, Hitler offered, in return for British non-intervention in Poland, to guarantee the British Empire, to provide German armed assistance when necessary, and to limit further growth of German armaments. Later the same day, during a meeting with the French Ambassador, Hitler heard that the Pact of Mutual Assistance between Britain and Poland had actually been signed in London. His attempt to isolate Poland had failed. Less than twelve hours before the deadline, the German invasion of Poland set for the 26th was halted.

President Franklin D. Roosevelt and Russian Foreign Minister Molotov during an informal meeting in the White House.
On 23rd August 1939, Molotov signed the Non-Aggression Pact with Germany in Moscow. Here Molotov signs for Russia.
Ribbentrop and Stalin are behind him.

Left: Hitler and Field Marshal Walther von Brauchitsch attend manoeuvres of the Second Army Corps in August 1938. Hitler's close personal interest in matters military rapidly got out of hand after the beginning of the war, when he moved on from matters of strategy, in which he showed great skill and occasional brilliance, to those of tactics, in which his acute lack of command experience became a grievous handicap to the generals whose opinions he frequently and increasingly ignored.

Right: Hitler on manoeuvres again, this time with Colonel-General Heinz Guderian, creator of the Panzer (tank) divisions and the leading advocate of armoured warfare in the Wehrmacht. Promoted Commander of the 16th Army Corps in February 1938, Guderian played a major role in Hitler's bloodless occupations of Austria and the Sudetenland. He commanded the 19th Panzer Corps from August 1939 to May 1940, achieving great success in Poland and France, and subsequently had more success on the Eastern Front until relieved of his command in December 1941.

Below: Hitler took great pleasure in meeting his officers and sharing the more pleasurable side of military life.

143

Above left: In June 1940, Hitler poses wth the parachutist heroes of the glider attack on Fort Eben Emael, a fortress on the junction of the Meuse and the Albert Canal in Belgium. Eighty men under the command of a sergeant landed in nine gliders on the roof of the fort and in thirty hours silenced its guns and made possible the capture of 1,200 defenders on May 11th 1940.

Below left: Hitler in more ceremonial surroundings taking the salute at a march past of the Black Guards.

Above: Hitler salutes the fallen of the Great War at the memorial in the Unter Den Linden, Berlin. This annual ceremony, 'Heroes Day', was used by Hitler to underline his constantly reiterated message that Germany's humiliation by the Treaty of Versailles must be avenged.

Right : When the opportunity to avenge the Versailles humiliation came, Hitler made the most of it. He had the original Armistice railway carriage brought from its Paris museum home back to the Forest of Compiegne, and obliged the French to sign the armistice in it, as Germany had done in 1918. Three days later, Hitler had the nearby memorial tablet commemorating the previous armistice blown up. Here we see Hitler touring Paris – his sole visit to the French capital.

The slide into war.

itler was now visibly showing the great strain that was upon him. Observers reported his looking older, and more haggard. He had only three courses open to him. The first was to try and recreate the situation that led to Munich – political pressure from Britain on the Poles to surrender in order to avoid a wider conflict. The second was to attempt to make the Poles' obstinacy the means of driving a wedge between Poland and Britain. The third was a lightning attack on Poland that would be over before Britain and France were able to respond to it. He kept all three options fully open throughout the nine days that elapsed before the outbreak of war on September 3rd.

Although less cool under stress than he had once been, Hitler remained resolute. On the 27th, he set a deadline of September 1st for the invasion of Poland. On the 28th, Britain formally declined Hitler's offer to protect the British Empire, and advised Hitler that both Britain and Poland were prepared to meet for negotiations. Hitler, wrongly, interpreted this as a sign of weakening resolve, and characteristically increased the stakes. He demanded that a Polish emissary be sent to Berlin on the following day with full powers to negotiate and settle. To do that, Poland would have inevitably to accept surrender, just as the Austrians and Czechs had done before. The Poles refused.

Hitler now, with total and mindbending hypocrisy, cast the Poles in the role of being the only obstacle to peaceful settlement of the Danzig question – he tried to drive the wedge between Poland and her allies. On the 30th August, Germany's claims against Poland were put into writing, incredibly enough, for the first time. Under sixteen heads, the claims included the return of Danzig, an internationally controlled plebiscite on the Polish Corridor, extra-territorial communications across the corridor and an exchange of populations. Henderson tried to get the Poles to the negotiating table to discuss the sixteen points. Poland again refused.

At dawn on September 1st, the date set down in Hitler's directive as long before as April 1939, the guns opened fire on Poland, the armies moved forward, and war became virtually inevitable. This time the German people did not rejoice as they had in 1914. Hitler found himself on the defensive as he addressed the Reichstag. The honeymoon with Germany was over.

Hitler now waited anxiously to see what Britain and France would do. Diplomatic sources told him of frantic comings and goings between embassies in London and Paris. Then at 9am on the morning of September 3rd, Henderson delivered an ultimatum from Britain. Hitler's worst fears were confirmed. Chamberlain and Britain were not backing down. The ultimatum said that, unless satisfactory assurances of German action to call off the attack on Poland were received by 11am, a state of war would exist between Britain and Germany.

Hitler was not a man to lose face by retreating. And thus it was that there was no assurance, and that Neville Chamberlain broadcast that morning to the British people telling them that they were once more at war with Germany. As in Germany, the message was received in reflective silence. For this was a war that nobody, not even the man who caused it, actually wanted.

Mussolini shakes hands with Daladier of France, with Hitler and Chamberlain in the background after the signing of the Munich Agreement on September 29th 1938.

Hitler's confidence showed as he announced the success of the occupation of the Rhineland to Nazi Party leaders on 10th March 1936.

On 14th April 1939, a week after Italy's invasion of Albania, President Roosevelt made a speech asking Hitler and Mussolini if they were willing to give assurances of non-aggression against thirty countries. Hitler's reply to the Reichstag at the Kroll Opera House on April 28th was probably the finest speech of his career, and was a masterpiece of ironic oratory. These pictures, taken on that historic day, show Hitler in full flood, using every trick of voice, gesture and expression to woo from the German people at the expense of Roosevelt the total support he knew he would soon need. Goering, who chaired the session as President of the Reichstag, was delighted; the many inaccuracies and lies of the text of Hitler's speech were overlooked. Hitler spoke of "the international warmongers in the democracies" who sought only to misrepresent Germany's intentions. He pointed out that the USA, whose President Roosevelt said differences could be resolved around the conference table, had demonstrated its belief in that principle by failing to join the League of Nations: he emphasised the birth of the USA in conflict, and the necessity of the American Civil War to create a united nation – and drew the inevitable conclusions.

Left: At the conclusion of the speech, which lasted more than two hours, the entire assembly rose and saluted Hitler with renewed patriotic fervour.

Right: The ever passive Rudolf Hess sits expressionless as his Fuehrer listens with rapt attention to the earlier proceedings of the Reichstag.

Listening intently in the Kroll Opera House to Hitler's famous speech of April 28th 1939 are Goebbels (left), Hess (right) and Ribbentrop (second from right). Two years later, Hitler addresses the Reichstag on 4th May 1941. Six weeks after this the attack on Russia began.

Success and conquest.

It must be beyond the scope of a short biography such as this to attempt to plot in any detail the course of the Second World War, which is in itself, even in outline, the subject matter for a much larger book. This book is about Hitler the man. So far, we have seen a paradoxical figure – successively an educational failure; an idler; a brave and successful if unappealing soldier; a verbose and yet charismatic revolutionary; a brilliant orator yet an appalling writer; an unparalleled master of political manoeuvre; a sadistic bigot; a lover of Wagner and fine architecture; a callous, vicarious murderer; and finally an occasionally unstable dictator whose increasingly unreasoning attitude to political problems divorced him more and more from the German people on the one hand and from those with whom he might negotiate on the other. Already in 1939 one can, with historical hindsight, detect the theatricality of Hitler's attitude to his own inevitable end.

Now, with the *Wehrmacht* attack on Poland smashing its way through to conquest and subjugation in a matter of only a fortnight or so, Hitler's fears about war seemed abruptly to vanish. He was again massively, overbearingly confident. He believed that there was no reason at all why Britain and France should remain at war once the Polish question was settled, since it was in his view inevitable that they should recognise his invincibility. Nor had his political cunning yet deserted him. On 6th October 1939 he made a speech that seemed to contain a peace offer – and when Chamberlain rejected it a week later, Hitler claimed that Britain was responsible for the continuation of the war.

Above: *Hitler beams in Asch after the occupation of the Sudetenland in 1938 – his confidence was hit by Britain's stand over Poland, but returned as his Blitzkrieg triumphed.*

Right: *The sinister caption to this picture, as issued by the Reich Propaganda Ministry reads: "Now Poland is being purged of Jews. Here we see armed guards with fixed bayonets searching from house to house in Warsaw."*

Hitler now had to eliminate French and German opposition before fulfilling his own prophecy in *Mein Kampf* by turning East to Russia. He began to be more and more introspective, much more involved in strategic planning, conferences and decisions. He was seen in public much less frequently. He began to assert himself much more forcefully against his generals, who saw no reason to extend the war in the West, perhaps because they did not realise the extent of Hitler's intentions in the East. The more he attempted to direct the war, the more he proved his temperamental unsuitability for military command, by his excitability, his tendency always to blame others and his timewasting verbosity.

By winter 1939-1940, the Pact of Steel was unpopular in both Germany and Italy. Russia was supplying huge quantities of vital food and raw materials, and Hitler deferred to Stalin at almost every turn, alienating Mussolini's always volatile affections as he did so. But as a result, Hitler was able to put virtually all his armed might on the Western Front, keeping only seven divisions in the East. Goering estimated after the war that the Russian pact was worth fifty divisions to Hitler in 1940.

Hitler's attack in the West was deferred several times during the 'phoney war,' and it was Russia's attack on Finland in December 1939, and the consequent threat to Swedish iron ore supplies that caused Hitler to consider the invasion of Norway as an adjunct to his main plan to sweep through Holland, the Ardennes and coastal France to the Channel, cutting off the British and France from the sea. In April, Norway was captured with superb surprise, and on 10th May, 89 German divisions swept into the Low Countries for the long awaited attack in the West. The speed of the collapse of Holland and Belgium surprised even Hitler. By the 17th May, "the Fuehrer is terribly nervous; frightened by his own success" (General Halder). As a result, Hitler stopped General Guderian's advance for two days, and the British army gained enough breathing space to make it to the sea at Dunkirk, and be evacuated to Britain. This was Major Blunder Number One of several that could be argued to have cost Hitler the war.

In mid-June, France was beaten, Reynaud resigned and Petain established the puppet government of Vichy, signing on June 22nd an armistice in the very railway carriage in which the hated armistice of 1918 had been completed. Hitler had gone to enormous trouble to get the carriage from the museum in Paris, to set it up in the Forest of Compiegne exactly as it had been in 1918, and to emphasise the completeness of his triumph. Germany had overrun Norway, Denmark, Holland, Belgium, Luxembourg, and France, and had driven the British into the sea. Hitler's political triumphs before the war stand comparison with Bismarck, his military victories early in the war with Napoleon. Both were due to his greatest single ability, that of being able to pinpoint and exploit the weaknesses of his opponents.

Once more, Hitler expected Britain to sue for peace. Once more he was disappointed. Throughout the summer of 1940, as the Battle of Britain raged in the air, Hitler planned Operation Sealion, the invasion of England. But Sealion depended on control of the air by the *Luftwaffe,* which Goering had been unable to provide. In October, Sealion was postponed indefinitely, and Hitler went fatally against his own tactical decision to triumph totally in the West before he turned East. He grossly underestimated Britain's ability to recover and fight back.

The drive for new achievement.

itler was, at the beginning of 1941, intensely frustrated. His grand plan in the West had gone brilliantly, and yet he had fallen short of the final conquest of Britain. He was planning the conquest of Russia – and had been so doing for months – but could not make a move. And, worst of all, his position as sole arbiter of military strategy had been usurped by Mussolini who had, in October 1940, unnecessarily and unwisely invaded Greece; had found himself in difficulties and had opened up a new theatre of war.

Molotov, Russia's Foreign Minister, was proving to be Hitler's first opponent to be totally unmoved by his theatricality and oratory, and the first successfully to upstage him in diplomacy. Japan had declined to make an immediate attack on Singapore to stretch Britain's resources. And Italy's war in North Africa against the British was proving a disaster from which Germany, as in Greece, was having to rescue her. Hitler now began to rely on his military rather than his political abilities, and thereby turned his back on his greatest asset.

In April 1941, alarmed at Soviet incursions in the Balkans, Hitler attacked Yugoslavia, which capitulated on April 17th. On the 23rd, Greece finally abandoned resistance to the Germans. Between March 31st and 12th April, Field Marshal Erwin Rommel, one of the most charismatic figures of the war, made a dazzling advance across North Africa almost to Egypt, thus disposing of British gains against the Italians. Germany was now in an immensely strong position in the Mediterranean theatre of war. One swift attack could entirely destroy the British presence in the Middle East and secure Hitler relief from one major theatre of

war. Hitler's generals urged him to take his chance.

But Hitler had determined almost a year before that he would attack Russia in the summer of 1941, and succeed where Napoleon failed by subjugating the USSR by October. Unwilling to be confused by facts or reason, Hitler deferred finishing the Mediterranean war until October, when he believed Russia would be defeated. He thereby lost his chance of victory in North Africa. It was his Major Blunder Number Two.

Major Blunder Number Three came on 22nd June when the German Army and Air Force set out to realise Hitler's dream, set out explicitly in *Mein Kampf,* of "liberating Russia from Soviet Jewry." The blunder was to embark on this campaign, Barbarossa, which was militarily unnecessary, while Germany was already occupied extensively elsewhere, and while there was potential for further battles on Continental Europe when Britain was ready. Having made the attack, and committed a huge army to the conquest, Hitler made matters worse by insisting on personal military control of operations. The generals, having achieved impressive inroads into Russian territory in the first weeks, wanted to push on to Moscow and complete the conquest by overcoming the capital. Hitler insisted on a broad front, and wanted to clear Russia from the Baltic states (Latvia, Lithuania, Estonia) and capture Leningrad before going on to Moscow. Initially, Hitler rejected the army's view, then later gave up the Leningrad adventure, although not before he had wasted so much time that winter was coming, and the advance was slowed at a critical time. By October 1941, the Germans were bogged down well short of their objective.

Far left: *The German Propaganda Ministry caption to this picture stated that it showed General Erwin Rommel 'taking refreshment in Tobruk, after the evacuation by the British forces.' Rommel it is, but Tobruk it almost certainly is not. The dazzling Afrika Korps drive across Cyrenaica in the first half of April 1941 established the Rommel legend.*

Left: *Conditions on the Eastern Front were truly appalling for the German Army, which had embarked on the Russian campaign ill-equipped for the harshness of the winter conditions.*

Below: *Hitler and Mussolini pictured visiting an unspecified location on the Eastern Front.*

A 1944 picture that gives some idea of the appalling conditions suffered by German troops during the Russian winter. Morale was low as it became clear that Germany could not win in Russia.

itler now concentrated his strategic and tactical energies almost exclusively on the war in the East, and spent most of his time at the *Wolfsschanze* (Wolf's Lair) near Rastenburg in East Prussia, visiting Berlin only occasionally. Yet he made it to Munich for the traditional 8th November celebrations on the anniversary of the Beer Cellar putsch. Hitler now became yet more introspective and broody as his great enterprise stagnated in the cold of a Russian winter. More than one visitor to the Wolf's Lair remarked how the gloom of the concrete headquarters amid the forest made even the most optimistic caller feel depressed. Yet Hitler still saw the new German Empire as being established in Russia.

On 6th December, the Russians counter-attacked as the advance units of the German Army were within sight of Moscow. The severely demoralised and very cold German Army – thousands of German soldiers had died of cold because Hitler had obstinately refused to supply winter uniforms for the campaign that was to be over by October – almost ran for home. But by appealing to old loyalties, imposing severe disciplinary measures and leaning on the Army's oath to the Fuehrer, Hitler held the line. The very next day, Japan attacked Pearl Harbour and brought America into the war. As a reprisal for Hitler's failing to inform Japan of the attack on Russia – a fact which brought down the Japanese government of the day – Japan neglected to

tell Hitler in advance about Pearl Harbour. Greatly under-estimating US determination and strength – perhaps fooled by America's several Neutrality Acts – Hitler declared war on the USA, and thereby perpetrated Major Blunder Number Four.

From this time on, there was no German High Command capable of independent action. Hitler demonstrated increasingly that, although he had considerable gifts as a strategist and was a master of surprise and psychological effect, he had none of the benefits conferred by experience of command in the field. Having taken supreme power, he had nobody left to blame. The unbearable pressures of failure began to wear Adolf Hitler down. In March 1942, Goebbels expressed shock at Hitler's appearance when he saw him for the first time in many weeks, describing him as quite grey and very aged. Hitler was complaining of bouts of giddiness, and was less than ever willing to listen to advice. Ever capable of convincing himself of false truths, he became more than ever the victim of his own propaganda.

In February 1942, Hitler appointed Albert Speer Minister of Armaments and Munitions, and thereby acquired one of the few truly professional and able administrators ever to be in his governmental team. Within months, Speer brought about enormous increases in aircraft and armaments production, without which Germany's war could not have continued. This appointment was the major factor in holding together the

German war effort during the two years that Hitler concentrated on the war in the East. But by mid-1943, nonetheless, Hitler's armies were outnumbered and outgunned by the Allies, and never recovered their supremacy.

Things were going badly in Russia as the second winter of the campaign gripped the German Army in its terrible cold. In the Autumn, the Germans had been halted at Stalingrad. Despite desperate fighting by the Sixth Army under General Paulus, by the end of January 1943 they were surrounded and had perforce to surrender to the Russians. Paulus and others of his staff were taken prisoner.

Germany had also suffered reverses in North Africa. On the 23rd of October, General Montgomery's newly inspired 8th Army had broken out at El Alamein and begun the advance that was to culminate in the driving out of the Axis forces from North Africa. And in the summer of 1943, Russia launched a massive counter-offensive that was not to end until they reached Berlin.

Early in the war, Hitler had squandered his advantage with which he could undoubtedly have won had he listened to his generals. Now, in mid-1943, he was still fighting the war he had planned in 1939-40, not the war that events had forced upon him. Already, Hitler was beginning to live in a fantasy world.

Above: Albert Speer, Minister of Armaments Production and Head of the Todt Organisation, which provided slave labour for the building of fortifications, visiting the Eastern Front. Despite his non-political background as an architect, Speer was Hitler's best ministerial appointment.

Below: General Friedrich Paulus, commander of the German Sixth Army, hopefully promoted Field Marshal by Hitler on the eve of the surrender at Stalingrad on the macabre grounds that no German Field Marshal had ever been captured. It did not work. Paulus and the remains of his proud army surrendered on January 30th 1943.

Rearguard detachments of the German Army in the Caucasus screen their comrades' evacuation from the next Russian thrust in February 1943.

The summer of 1943 also saw relationships with Italy badly strained. On 10th July, the Allies landed in Sicily, and on the 25th, the King of Italy dismissed Mussolini, who was placed under arrest, and replaced by Badoglio. Hitler's immediate wish was to stage a coup d'état to re-establish his ally, but he thought better of it. On September 8th, the Italians signed an Armistice with the allies, which brought Hitler, once a frequent broadcaster to the German people, to the microphone for the first time since March, when he had made a terrible, rambling, poorly presented speech. Some of his old fire had returned in the face of the Italian situation, but his oratory lacked all its former brilliance. On 12th September, the *Waffen SS* rescued Mussolini spectacularly from the mountains of Italy, and brought him to Hitler at Berchtesgaden. Hitler proclaimed the 'Italian Social Republic' with Mussolini at its head, but it was an empty gesture born of fantasy.

In Russia, the Germans were being pushed back fast, and the political effect on the population of Germany, especially in the East, was considerable. Hitler's popularity waned sharply, as people realised that Germany was losing the war. But Hitler would have none of it, and Goebbels' propaganda broadcasts maintained a spirit of optimism. Hitler was now suffering from trembling of the right arm and leg, and dragged his left foot. Explanations then and since have varied from diagnoses of Parkinsons Disease to speculations about tertiary syphilis. The Fuehrer was taking increasing doses of quite terrifying drugs

prescribed by a Dr Morell – the principal mixture was one of strychnine and belladonna. His conversation had become more than ever repetitious, and his life hermit-like and secretive. Goebbels, after a visit, wrote in his diary, "It is tragic that the Fuehrer has become such a recluse and leads such an unhealthy life . . . He sits in his bunker, worries and broods." Increasingly, Hitler's fantasy world was taking over. He refused to visit bombed cities, or to see or discuss any aspect of the war that did not conform to his idealised notion of it. Wrote Goebbels in September 1943, "He is guided by hatred, not by reason."

Events continued to go against Germany as 1944 succeeded 1943. The Normandy invasion of June 1944 opened up the Western Front once more, and, with Russia hammering in from the East, the end was in sight. On 20th July 1944, Count von Stauffenberg almost succeeded in assassinating Hitler at the Wolf's Lair as part of an elaborate revolutionary plan, but Hitler, almost miraculously, escaped with quite minor wounds although others near him were killed and seriously injured. His response to the plot was ruthless. Nearly 5,000 people were executed, including Stauffenberg himself.

On 11th September the Americans set foot in Germany, and Hitler's war had come home on land – although the appallingly devastating bombing by the RAF by night and the US Air Forces by day had long terrorised the populations of the German cities. But still the German Army fought well. The Allied Airborne expedition to Arnhem was a sad failure, and the German 15th

Army held Antwerp far longer than expected, not losing it until November. On 24th August, Hitler had ordered total mobilisation of the German population. Every male from 16 to 60 was under arms. In September, Hitler and Jodl planned the Ardennes offensive –the Battle of the Bulge – destined to be Germany's last great thrust and demonstration of its former might.

Although initially impressive, the Ardennes offensive never really broke through, and by 8th January, 1945, Hitler agreed to withdraw the armour. The Germans suffered 120,000 casualties in the battle, the Americans 77,400. On 12th January, 180 Russian divisions attacked in Poland, and by the end of the month Marshal Zhukov was less than 100 miles from Berlin.

Above left: A picture by the famous photographer Robert Capa of officers of a crack SS regiment captured by the US 2nd Armoured Division between Granvilles and Avranches in Normandy after the invasion of June 1944.

Above: A group of German parachute troops captured during the storming of Brest by the allies. The German Army paratroops were tough and well trained, but morale was flagging by late 1944.

Hitler seemed to lead a charmed life in his dealings with would-be assassins.

Above left: Just after Hitler had left the annual commemoration of the Munich Beer Cellar Putsch on November 9th 1939, somebody blew up the cellar.

Right: Martin Bormann (left), Goering (3rd from left) and others inspect the damage after the 1944 explosion.

Below left: Wirmer, Bruning's secretary, on trial for his life after the Stauffenberg plot. He was executed.

Below right: Count Schwern and Schwanenfeld on trial. He too was executed.

164

Above left: The devastation inside Hitler's 'Wolf's Lair' at Rastenburg after the Stauffenberg bomb plot of 20th July 1944.

Below: The scene in the People's Court during the trial of those implicated in the Stauffenberg bomb plot.

Above: Hitler and Colonel-General Alfried Jodl at Rastenburg before the bomb plot.

Right: (Left to right) Martin Bormann, Colonel-General Jodl and A. Bormann, Martin's brother, with Hitler after the Stauffenberg bomb. Notice Hitler holding his semi-paralysed right arm.

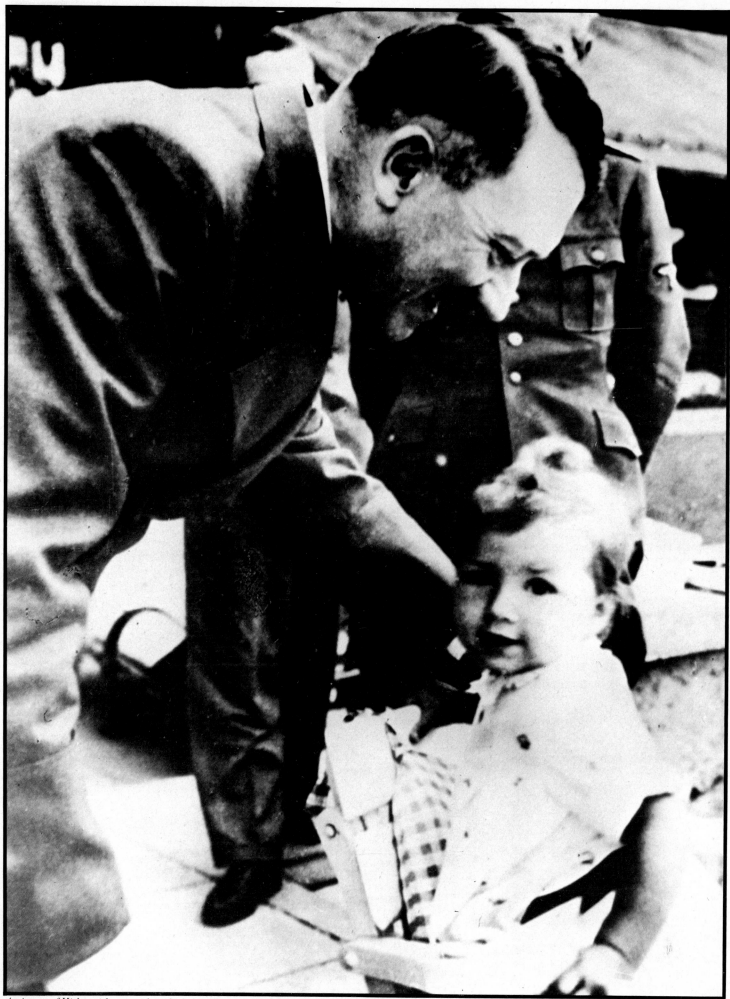

A picture of Hitler with an unidentified child that was found by American troops among Eva Braun's possessions, and which gave rise to speculation that this could be Hitler's child.

Another shot from one of Eva Braun's photograph albums, this time almost certainly of 'Uschi,' Eva Braun's niece. This picture was found in Frankfurt.

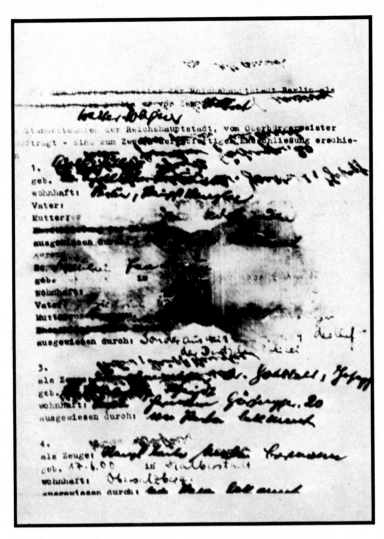

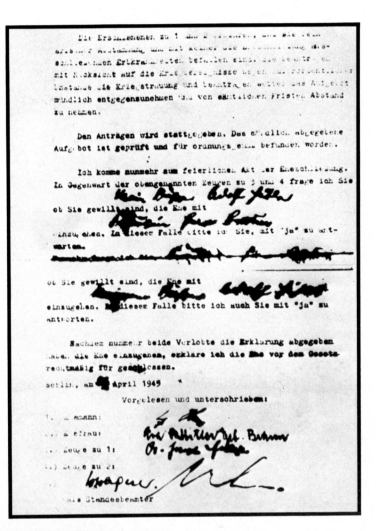

Below: The second page of the marriage certificate. Towards the bottom can be seen the signatures of Adolf Hitler (the first signature) and of Eva Braun. The lower signatures are those of the witnesses. In the same suitcase that produced the certificate was found Hitler's will.

Above: The first page of Hitler's and Eva Braun's marriage certificate, damaged by fire and water, which was found in a battered suitcase in Tegernsee, a lake some 30 miles from Munich. The certificate was seized by US Third Army Intelligence officers when they arrested Martin Bormann's adjutant, Frederick Paustin.

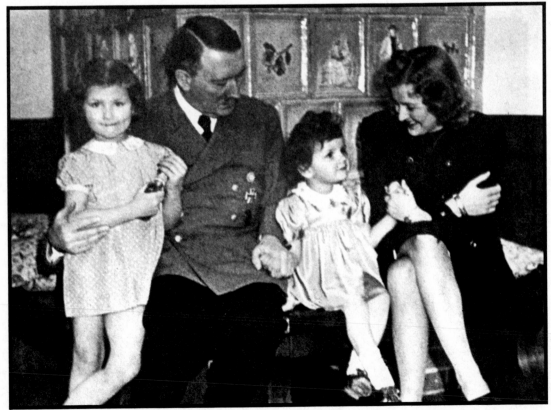

Far left: This picture, ingenuously titled 'Hitler and friend' by a New York picture editor in November 1945, shows Hitler and Eva Braun, then his mistress, at Berchtesgaden. Like the pictures on the previous page, this was found among Eva Braun's possessions.

Left: Nearing the end of his life, Hitler poses with Eva Braun and two little girls who are not named – but the girl on the right is almost certainly Eva Braun's niece Uschi.

Above: Hitler and Eva Braun (right) at Berchtesgaden with Frau Morell, the wife of Hitler's physician Dr Theodor Morell. The good doctor was something of a quack, and had gradually caused drug addiction in Hitler as a result of endless prescriptions of 'medicinal pills'.

Right: Although photographed several times with German Shepherd Dogs, Hitler was virtually never seen with other breeds. This picture is an exception, photographed at Berchtesgaden, although whose dogs they were is not recorded. Perhaps Eva Braun was showing him her idea of a dog?

Far right: A picture released on Hitler's 55th and final birthday on April 20th 1944 shows him with Blondi, the German Shepherd Dog that Martin Bormann gave him as a birthday present.

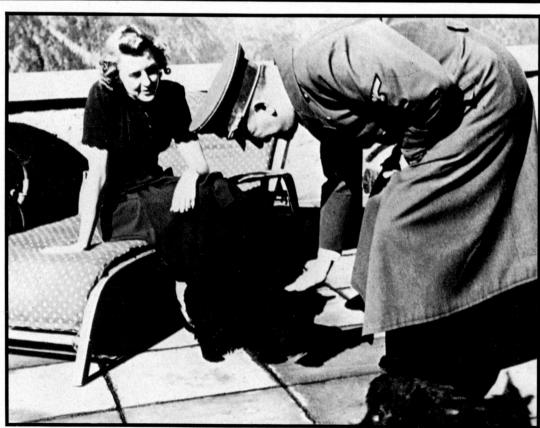

A saddened Hitler, who had boasted that German territory would never be bombed, on one of his rare visits to the devastation wrought by allied bombers.

Above left: *A young Russian soldier sits on the sofa upon which Hitler is reputed to have shot himself. When the Russians broke into the bunker, they found the place waterlogged.*

Above right: *Intriguingly, this picture is also captioned as 'a Russian soldier on the bed in the Fuehrer's shelter where Hitler and Eva Braun are alleged to have poisoned themselves'. Since Hitler shot himself, the probability is that it was on this bed that Eva Braun died of poison, and Hitler died on the bed in the other picture.*

A Russian **facing page, top** *uses Eva Braun's phone in her bedroom in the bunker.*

Below: *A group of war correspondents in the garden of the ruined Berlin Chancellery in May 1945 are shown the grave in which Hitler's charred body was alleged to have been buried. Some feeling of truth is lent to this picture by the petrol cans that are still beside the pit, but the whole episode of Hitler's body and its disposal was and is shrouded in confusion and misinformation.*

The remains of Hitler's Rastenburg headquarters 'The Wolf's Lair', **facing page, bottom** *now a tourist attraction.*

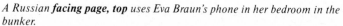

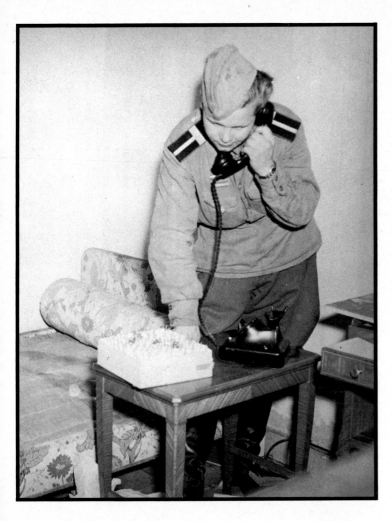

In mid-January, Hitler had moved back to the Chancellery in Berlin where he was now to stay for the rest of his life. In February, Captain Gerhard Boldt, attending a conference, noted that "His head was slightly wobbling . . . His face and the parts around his eyes gave the impression of total exhaustion. All his movements were those of a senile man." Hitler now began to drop the veneer of culture that power had brought to him, and once again spoke and acted like the down and out that he had been in his youth. There was nobody left to impress. He trusted only his mistress Eva Braun, and his dog Blondi, an Alsatian bitch given to him by Martin Bormann during the previous year.

On the 12th April, the Americans crossed the Elbe. There was no longer any organised direction of German government, nor of the war. Hitler had lost his grasp of the situation, and gave orders for deliberate brutality to the enemy which were often ignored. On 22nd April, as the Russians broke through into Berlin, Hitler announced, with Eva Braun at his side in the bunker, that he would not go South to continue the fight and direct his remaining troops, but would stay and die in Berlin. Thus, at the hour when his armies and people needed leadership most, Hitler deserted Germany. Just as he had done in the 1923 putsch, he abdicated responsibility when the going got tough.

On 26th April, the bunker was shelled. The end could not be far away. On the 29th, he summoned a municipal official, and ordered him to conduct his marriage to Eva Braun. He appointed Admiral Doenitz his successor – angering Goering, who had earlier sent a telegram asking for the job in the light of his appointment as Deputy Fuehrer years before. The next day, after a good lunch, Hitler and his wife of less than a day went to one of the private rooms in the bunker. One shot was heard. Goebbels and Bormann went to the room and found that Hitler had shot himself through the mouth. Eva had taken poison, and was also dead.

Always aware of the importance of due ceremony, Hitler had left detailed instructions for the disposal of the bodies, and they were carried out precisely. Both bodies were taken up to the garden of the Chancellery, soaked in petrol and burned. It was twelve years and three months to the day since Hitler had become Chancellor. Goebbels kept the deaths secret for a day, and then announced them on the radio on May 1st, saying that Hitler had died heroically at the head of his troops.

The Third Reich, proclaimed by Hitler as to last for a thousand years, outlasted its founder by only one week. The Russians had conquered East Germany and were in Berlin: their continued presence there and throughout Eastern Europe is Hitler's most enduring legacy. Millions had died in the cause of an evil dream that turned to a nightmare. It happened because the German people, faced with unpalatable realities in the aftermath of war, chose to follow a plausible charlatan who promised – and then seemingly delivered – the impossible.

That Hitler wrought the greatest act of genocide the world has known is undisputable. That he was a genius of political manoeuvre is almost above discussion. He was at one time the greatest leader, the greatest achiever, and the greatest evil of the twentieth century. Few, if any centuries have seen a man who can be compared with him in all those characteristics. It may yet prove that Adolf Hitler was the greatest paradox of history.